EXHIBITING STUDENT ART

EXHIBITING STUDENT ART

The Essential Guide for Teachers

David Burton

FOREWORD BY TERRY BARRETT

TEACHERS COLLEGE PRESS

TEACHERS COLLEGE | COLUMBIA UNIVERSITY

NEW YORK AND LONDON

Published by Teachers College Press, 1234 Amsterdam Avenue, New York, NY 10027

The author gratefully acknowledges permission for the use of quoted material and photographs from the following sources: Association for Supervision and Curriculum Development (P. Koetsch et al., "Schools into Museums," *Educational Leadership*, 2002), National Association for the Education of Young Children (D. Diffily, "The Project Approach: A Museum Exhibit Created by Kindergartners," *Young Children*, 1996), National Art Education Association (C. Davis, Ed., "NAEA Policy on Contests and Competitions," *Advisory NAEA*, 1998; G. Szekely "The Display Art of Children," 2001; and D. Burton and T. McGraw, "Students as Curators," 2001), and Jennifer Cross and the Ross School for material from various exhibition catalogs. We deeply appreciate photographs supplied by Robert Sabol, Ralph Caouette, Autumn Sears Fesperman, Sherry Snowden, the New Art Center, and Jennifer Cross and the Ross School.

Library of Congress Cataloging-in-Publication Data

Burton, David.
    Exhibiting student art : the essential guide for teachers / David Burton.
      p. cm.
    Includes bibliographical references and index.
    ISBN-13: 978-0-8077-4673-8 (cloth : alk. paper)
    ISBN-13: 978-0-8077-4672-1 (pbk. : alk. paper)
    ISBN-10: 0-8077-4673-8 (cloth : alk. paper)
    ISBN-10: 0-8077-4672-X (pbk. : alk. paper)
    1. Children's art—United States. 2. Schools—United States—Exhibitions.
  3. Art—Exhibition techniques. I. Title.

    N352.2.U6B87 2005
    704.083'4075—dc22

                                            2005055945

ISBN-13:	ISBN-10:
978-0-8077-4672-1 (paper)	0-8077-4672-X (paper)
978-0-8077-4673-8 (cloth)	0-8077-4673-8 (cloth)

Printed on acid-free paper

Manufactured in the United States of America

For my wife,

Theresa Bailey Burton,

"Mrs. Bailey,"

who inspires me.

Contents

Foreword by *Terry Barrett*   xi

Acknowledgments   xiii

Introduction   **1**
The Five Steps of Exhibition   2
Social Dynamics of Exhibiting Student Art   4
Recognizing the Benefits of Student Art Exhibitions   6

**Part I   Involving Students in the
Art Exhibition Process**

Chapter 1   Theme Development   **11**
Curating a Theme   11
Teamwork and Consensus Building   12
Categories of Themes   14
Developing Criteria from Themes   21
Selecting Art   24
Conclusion   27

Chapter 2   Exhibition Design   **29**
Designing an Exhibition   30
Installation Designs   33
Developing an Exhibition Brief   39
An Exhibition Timetable and Checklist   41
Using a Scale Model of the Exhibition Space   44
Conclusion   45

Chapter 3   Exhibition Installation   **47**
Accessioning Art for Exhibition   47
Preparing Art for Exhibition   49

Preparing the Site for Exhibition   50
Selecting a Title for the Exhibition   53
Creating Signage and Text   54
Arranging and Installing the Art   55
Interactive Installation: The Viewer Plays an Active Role   59
Event or Performance: Create a Fantasy   60
Ambience   61
Conclusion   61

Chapter 4   Exhibition Publicity   **64**

A Shift in Perspective: Taking the Viewer's Point of View   64
Cultivating an Audience   65
Advertising: Romancing the Show   66
Exposition   68
Conclusion   72

Chapter 5   Exhibition Events and Assessment   **74**

The Reception   74
Maintaining the Exhibition   79
Aftermath: Dismantling the Show   80
Exhibition as Authentic Assessment   80
Assessing the Exhibition   81
Conclusion   85

Chapter 6   Teaching Art Exhibition   **86**

The Role of the Teacher: Facilitator, Supervisor, Instructor   86
Developing an Exhibition Program   87
Working with an Artist   88
Juried Shows and Competitions   89
Originality   90
Controversial Art   90
Legal Considerations   94
Developing Support for Exhibitions   96
Turning Empty Spaces into Places for Art   99
Conclusion   107

PART II   A GALLERY OF CASES

Cases 1   Theme Development   **111**

Case 1.1   Art Exhibition with a Descriptive Theme   111
Case 1.2   Art Exhibition with a Narrative Theme   112

Case 1.3 Student Art Exhibition with a Metaphorical Theme   *114*
Case 1.4 Student Art Exhibition with an Emotive Theme   *114*
Case 1.5 Student Art Exhibition with an Honorific Theme   *116*
Case 1.6 Student Art Exhibition with an Issue-Oriented Theme   *117*
Case 1.7 Third Graders Selecting Art for an Exhibition   *118*

Cases 2   Exhibition Design   **120**

Case 2.1 Student Art Exhibition with a Salon-Style Design   *120*
Case 2.2 Art Exhibition with a Linear Installation Design   *121*
Case 2.3 Art Exhibition with a Sequential Installation Design *121*
Case 2.4 Student Art Exhibition with a Comparative
            Installation Design   *122*
Case 2.5 Art Exhibition with a Synoptic Installation Design   *123*
Case 2.6 Art Exhibition with a Contextual Installation Design *124*

Cases 3   Exhibition Installation   **126**

Case 3.1 Selecting and Installing Art   *126*
Case 3.2 Installing Student Art   *127*
Case 3.3 Developing an Interactive Installation   *128*
Case 3.4 Creating Ambience   *128*

Cases 4   Exhibition Publicity   **130**

Case 4.1 Planning Exhibition Publicity   *130*
Case 4.2 Example of a Student Review   *131*
Case 4.3 Interviewing and Writing an Apologia   *132*
Case 4.4 Preparing an Exhibition Catalog   *133*

Cases 5   Exhibition Events and Assessment   **134**

Case 5.1 Planning an Exhibition with an Opening Event   *134*
Case 5.2 Assessing Student Learning Through Art Exhibition   *135*

Cases 6   Teaching Art Exhibition   **137**

Case 6.1 Working with an Artist   *137*
Case 6.2 Leasing Student Art   *138*
Case 6.3 Exhibiting in School Hallways   *138*
Case 6.4 Exhibiting in a School Gallery   *139*
Case 6.5 Exhibiting at School Events and Community
            Events Held at School   *140*
Case 6.6 Exhibiting Throughout the School—Gallery Owners   *140*
Case 6.7 Exhibiting Between Schools—The Global Art Exchange   *141*
Case 6.8 Exhibiting Art Borrowed from Museums   *143*

Case 6.9   Exhibiting in the Community   *144*
Case 6.10   Exhibiting on a Web Site   *145*

Appendix   **NAEA Policy on Contests and Competitions**   **147**

References   **151**

Index   **155**

About the Author   **162**

Foreword

In this book, David Burton shows us how to bring art that students make in art rooms to more public spaces within schools and local communities. By doing this, we greatly expand the joy and enlightenment that student art can provide. *Exhibiting Student Art* is an important contribution to practice that promotes active student learning in classroom communal activities for the benefit of the learners and the larger communities where they reside. Rather than relegate student artwork to crowded school walls or display it on home refrigerators—or worse, throw it in the trash—Professor Burton and the many teachers with whom he has collaborated show us how to expand audiences for student artistic expressions.

Burton demonstrates how to help our students become active participants in expanding a limited art world comprised only of students, their teachers, and perhaps their parents to broader, diversified areas. There is much valuable learning to be had for students, teachers, and their newly expanded audiences through Burton's actual experiences with and expansive spirit regarding the exhibition of student art.

In Burton's proposal, elementary, middle-school, and high school students prepare exhibitions of their own works of art. The potential for active learning by the art students is inspiring. In selecting works to be displayed, students must grapple with constructing and organizing themes by which they can select a work and place it within an intellectually coherent group. The process teaches them to make difficult but fair choices about inclusion and exclusion. They are occasionally challenged to rationally resolve conflicts over what some consider controversial art. Such discussions can help students learn to disagree respectfully and come to acquire skills of consensus-building, thereby preparing them for active participation in a democratic society.

Once works to be displayed have been selected, the student-exhibition designers must determine the advantages and limitations of a given exhibition space and use the space towards its greatest potential. They face the challenges of preparing works to be hung or otherwise displayed and installing them for maximum aesthetic appeal and expressive communicative possibilities. They determine what texts, if any, should accompany the exhibition and the individual works of art. They invent ways to publicize the exhibition and to build communal events around it for different audiences. Finally, they assess the effectiveness of what they have done so that they may learn from shortcomings and become motivated toward designing more effective exhibition experiences in the future.

Students taught well by teachers influenced by this book will joyfully discover that the artworks that they make have value to others because of their aesthetic appeal, the expression of thoughts and feelings, and the ways the students have made their personal experiences accessible to others through visual materials.

When students successfully transfer what they have learned from mounting their own exhibitions to looking at exhibitions in private galleries and public museums, their school experiences with art will extend into positively altered, lifelong interactions in many art worlds, with their children, and with others throughout their lives. Because of their early art learning, they will be more likely to alter their home environments more consciously and knowledgably. They will attend with more curiosity to how families and friends embellish their own living spaces. They will approach an art exhibition seeking its organizing theme and how this theme colors the meanings of each work. They will wonder about the exhibitor's criteria for selection: What is included and what is excluded and why? They will attend to printed information accompanying the exhibition and the artworks, and how it has been written and designed to shape the impressions of what they see. They will likely watch and overhear others looking at art, learning about people's different preferences and values. They will assess their own experiences of the art, and perhaps seek out what professional critics have written about it.

By having been involved in creating exhibitions of art, students will realize that all decisions—not just those concerning art—are based, more or less, on reasons. If teachers help them internalize the information Burton has provided in this book, students will be rightly wary of many decisions that are based on too few or merely arbitrary reasons; they will also be better prepared in their lives to recognize and celebrate careful and effective decision making.

Terry Barrett
The Ohio State University

Acknowledgments

I wish to gratefully thank all the teachers who contributed to this book through their examples, insights, and suggestions. Terry Bailey Burton, Jennifer Cross, Robert Sabol, Peggy Wood, Tammy McGraw, and Sherry Snowden, in particular, have helped in so many ways.

I also wish to thank Susan Liddicoat, Aureliano Vázquez, Jr., and the staff at Teachers College Press, for their continuing patience, professional insights, and wise counsel in shepherding this book through the publication process.

Introduction

Exhibiting student art is art education's best-kept secret. Most art teachers regularly display their students' art, but they don't talk about doing so. Although exhibition has tremendous potential for art programs, it is largely underused. A survey I conducted of instructional strategies used by secondary school art teachers reveals the importance of exhibiting student art (Burton, 2001). One question in the survey was, "What instructional strategies have you found to be effective in motivating and inspiring students in art?" Ninety-nine of the 177 respondents (56%) answered that "exhibiting student art" was *very effective*; another 57 (32%) found it *moderately effective*. Together, those teachers represent 88% of those answering the question, a percentage second only to that of teachers responding, "working with a wide variety of media and processes"—a studio strategy.

Another question from the same survey was, "What additional duties that require professional skills are you involved in at your school?" Once more, the response, "art exhibition," stood out. Again, 99 (56%) of the respondents identified it as a *very frequent* duty, while another 48 (27%) labeled it a *frequent* duty. Combined, they represent 83% of the respondents.

What do these responses tell us? A large majority (88%) of art teachers recognize that exhibiting art is an effective motivational strategy, yet 83%, an equally significant number, do all the work of actually mounting the shows. Exhibiting student art is clearly a highly motivational activity, but in many cases, the students are not actively involved, and the art teachers are doing all the work.

When students exhibit their own art, they learn concepts and skills that are important to a comprehensive understanding of art and aesthetics. Exhibition punctuates the creative, artistic process in a natural and fulfilling way. Exhibition expands the context within which art exists. Students see their work in a larger perspective, in relation to the work of others, without their being singled out, as frequently happens in critiques. They recognize the value of their art through the appreciation shown by the public.

This experience is deepened when students participate in the process of exhibiting their own art. If a well-meaning art teacher collects the art, prepares it for exhibition, and hangs the show him- or herself, the students miss out on a significant educational experience. Their learning depends on engaging in the exhibition process themselves, firsthand.

In *Exhibiting Student Art* I describe an educational process through which students can acquire insights into how other people perceive art. I explain each step in the exhibition process in such a way that teachers can easily assist students to understand the project and participate successfully. Together, the concepts constitute a rich, new perspective on art, and the skills extend students' abilities to deal with art. As Daisy McTighe, who teaches art in Columbia, Maryland, emphasizes, student participation in art exhibition "is an integral part of our program and serves as the culmination of the artistic experience/process" (personal correspondence, October 2002).

THE FIVE STEPS OF EXHIBITION

Art exhibitions, whether presented in schools by students or in galleries and museums by professional curators, progress through five steps:

1. Theme development
2. Design
3. Installation
4. Publicity
5. Event/Assessment

In *Exhibiting Student Art* I guide teachers and students through the exhibition process, breaking each step down into specific tasks and showing how they can be taught and learned. Beginning with simple formats and assignments, students gradually progress to more sophisticated skills and concepts. My descriptions of each phase are, in turn, supported by case studies that demonstrate how teachers have successfully applied these principles of art exhibition in their own classrooms.

Taken together, these five steps may seem daunting. In fact, initial exhibitions are usually very modest affairs in which children simply arrange their work and put it up in ways that intuitively appeal to them. As they engage in more exhibitions, themes begin to emerge naturally. More exhibitions lead to variations in installations, which in turn lead to the question of exhibition design. Later, publicity and receptions extend the exhibition horizon even further. Publicity anticipates the event; receptions celebrate it and lead to assessment. The exhibition process evolves, becoming more elaborate and sophisticated as the students grow into it. There is no need to rush it or expect too much prematurely.

Theme Development

During the first phase, students, working with their art teacher, identify an interesting theme that serves as the conceptual basis for the exhibition. In *Exhibiting Student Art* I identify six broad thematic formats—descriptive, didactic, metaphorical, emotive, honorific, and issue oriented—for students to pursue. Dozens of specific themes fall under each of these general headings.

Just as an artist's reasons for making art change from work to work, so does the type of theme that can best exemplify a body of art. Developing an appropriate theme for a particular body of art ensures that it will be presented to its best advantage. Everything that follows—design, installation, publicity, and event/assessment—therefore builds upon that thematic foundation. Criteria for selecting specific works of art, and the works themselves, get chosen based on the theme.

Design

A successful exhibition requires students to arrange their art in the best possible way in order to carry through the intent of the theme they chose. Deciding why, how, and where their art should be hung, and how viewers will respond to it, should not be left to chance. An effective exhibition design requires a good deal of deliberate thought. Just as the first step offered a variety of thematic formats, this step provides several broad design alternatives to consider. During this phase, students also draft detailed plans (or briefs) and timetables that guide them through the rest of the exhibition process.

Installation

During the third phase, the imagined vision takes physical form. This phase addresses the actual installation of the artwork in a specific space. The students, with their teacher's guidance, prepare their artwork and the exhibition space and hang the show. As their repertoire of exhibition designs branches out, their installations will become more varied and sophisticated.

Publicity

Publicity constitutes the fourth phase, although in many instances it begins as soon as the theme for the show is approved. Publicists pursue a twofold mission: They try to whet the public's appetite for the forthcoming exhibition through advertising, while at the same time attempting to bring forth the exhibition's meaning through reviews, catalogs, and other written material. Publicity entails a wide variety of skills and tasks, most of which involves writing.

Event/Assessment

Engaging the public is the crux of the opening event. When viewers "meet" the art, a friendly introduction generally helps. In the beginning, receptions can be both simple and brief, but students will find many ways to extend them. As shows become more elaborate, they require more advanced planning and preparation. Authentic assessment is a natural outcome of participation in the art exhibition process.

Many variations of these five steps will be explored in Part I, Chapters 1–5. Threaded through these chapters is a continuing scenario of a middle school art class preparing an exhibition of student work. Chapter 6 provides additional guidance to teachers and practical advice related to involving students in art exhibition. Cross-references in the chapters in Part I point readers to pertinent cases in Part II, which show how actual teachers have developed creative approaches to exhibiting by using various types of themes, installation designs, venues, publicity, and opening events.

Although the case studies are cited in the chapters to illustrate a specific aspect of the exhibition process, most case descriptions encompass the entire process. As they illustrate, students may develop exhibitions of their own work; the work of other students; and in some cases, the work of professional artists in their communities or local museums. Each of these experiences enhances the students' understanding of what exhibitions are all about and how they function.

SOCIAL DYNAMICS OF EXHIBITING STUDENT ART

Social dynamics run through every aspect of exhibiting art, from bringing together the art of many students into a visual and conceptual whole, to presenting the art to the public in the most satisfying manner. Making students the center of this process allows them to hone their social skills and adds vitality to the entire project. Students work hard toward success with their peers on any enterprise intended for other students, friends, and family.

As students become more deeply involved in exhibiting, their art teachers can employ social dynamics to provide a structured context in which students can shape their own goals, thoughts, and aspirations at every stage of the exhibition process. When skillfully arranged, art exhibitions present artwork under ideal social conditions, and in return, allow the exhibitors to bask in the warm glow of the public's praise. The entire process demands commitment, cooperation, and constructive interaction, moving toward a common goal. As McLean (1993) points out:

> Because of their complexity, exhibitions are inevitably produced by groups of people. No matter what role one plays, developing an exhibition is an act of collaboration. . . . No matter how they are organized, to function creatively and efficiently groups need: 1) an atmosphere of mutual respect where members listen and respond to each other, rather then simply react; 2) administrative support and a climate that makes it possible to take risks and make mistakes; 3) a sense of responsibility shared by every member of the group; 4) a clear structure for decision-making and conflict resolution; and 5) a compelling vision or goal. (pp. 40–41)

This short agenda speaks volumes. Many teachers make *respect* the pervasive rule for their classroom. Everything else is predicated on that single principle. For many, the school year begins with lessons that incorporate students' practicing respect for one another in words and actions, which can then be reinforced throughout the school year. Organizing exhibitions provides many settings where groups must work together toward a common goal and where acting respectfully toward one another is necessary and rewarded.

Administrative support and a climate in which it is possible to take risks and make mistakes underwrite a creative milieu. In this case, administrative support comes from the art teacher, directly, and from the school, school administration, and community indirectly. Support from the top is necessary if team members are to achieve success. Any qualms the art teacher or administrator may have resonate through the entire exhibition process. Through monitoring the exhibition process closely, checking decisions as they are made, and making changes as needed, the process can proceed forward, even with detours, while the art teacher remains confident of its success. When risks are taken, they should be controlled for anticipated problems with workable solutions. When mistakes occur, they can be kept small and corrected immediately and without placing blame.

In exhibiting student art, sharing responsibility and having a compelling vision or goal are inexorably intertwined. The vision or goal is expressed through an exhibition theme that all team members share. Once students are committed to the theme, their responsibility to realize it can be shared as well. Making the theme and its meaning very clear, therefore, becomes paramount.

Many schools offer classes in social skills that focus on decision making and conflict resolution—after students get into trouble. Exhibiting student art creates contexts in which all students may develop the same skills to achieve highly motivating outcomes before the fact. Moreover, students have a strong vested interest in realizing successful exhibitions—the approbation of their peers—that is vitally important to them. By learning and practicing clearly stated procedures for making collective decisions and resolving conflicts, students benefit in all aspects of their art education. Keeping the thematic goal in mind helps considerably. Reiterating the ideal of mutual respect facilitates compromise and consensus.

Social dynamics vary depending on the scale and venue of the exhibition. Students obviously need to hone their exhibition skills on smaller, more modest shows before tackling major projects. So, too, their ability to work with others cooperatively should be appropriate to the complexity of the exhibition task at hand.

RECOGNIZING THE BENEFITS OF STUDENT ART EXHIBITIONS

Exhibiting art completes the artistic cycle. When exhibition is a regular component of the art program, the entire art curriculum becomes more coherent and directed. Students are motivated and empowered by their own work. Aesthetics, art criticism, and art history flow through the exhibition. Ideas raised during the exhibition process become the basis for future studio projects and aesthetic discussions.

Carole Mohor, an art teacher from McDonough, Georgia, asserts that exhibition "most certainly influences my art curriculum and shows its value and one of its purposes, that of viewing it and adding beauty to the environment. The quality of their art does increase when students know I want to exhibit their work" (personal correspondence, November 2002).

Marilyn Gragnolati, who teaches art in Windsor Lock, Connecticut, reflects, "I think it is an important completion to the total art-learning process. Students need to see their work in the context of others and be viewed from afar as well as up close. It also invites the feedback of those who view it" (personal correspondence, October 2002).

Exhibitions make an art program visible right along with the art itself. When art is attractively presented, students, teachers, parents, and administrators take note and appreciate its value and meaning. People entering a school replete with art immediately understand that art (and the art program) are important there.

Klista Meis, an art teacher in Perry, Iowa, reports the public's reaction to her students' exhibitions this way: "Positive! Displaying students' work promotes art programs. When visitors and parents make positive comments to administrators, our program benefits" (personal correspondence, October 2002).

Barbara Morano, who teaches in Springfield, New Jersey, makes it clear that "we are the *visual arts*. I think it is imperative that we display as much student artwork as possible" (personal correspondence, October 2002).

A diversity of expressions, ideas, issues, and inquiries directly contributes to the cultural richness of the school and community. Even when visual art occupies our surroundings passively, its influence is inescapable. It forces us to look, think, feel, and question. When new visual experiences are presented regularly, students learn to read them better and expect more from our visual environment.

Part I

Involving Students in the
Art Exhibition Process

CHAPTER 1

Theme Development

Curators provide vision and leadership for an exhibition. They conceive the initial concept, formulate the theme, draft the brief and timetable, coordinate personnel and tasks, and oversee the entire operation. In most cases, curators think of the original idea from which the rest of the exhibition evolves. That idea may be vague in the beginning. It may be simply the desire to express a certain indefinable intuition or it may spring forth in an insightful flash. However curators are inspired, that initial idea must be stated so that others working on the exhibition can share its vision and be motivated by its intent. Ultimately, that idea must also become so clear and compelling that the public will discover its meaning when they view the exhibition.

CURATING A THEME

Within a school setting, the curators' role may be performed in different ways. All too often teachers assume the role of curator themselves. They define the theme and style of the show, coordinate committees, assign tasks, and personally supervise every aspect of the process. In fact, they may do all of the work themselves, including selecting the art, hanging the show, and finally dismantling it. While that strategy may be efficient, if students are not involved in the exhibition process, they learn very little from it.

Conversely, the entire class may act as curators. Young children especially enjoy this approach. Collectively, they can discuss many ideas for shows, develop a single theme through consensus, organize the various tasks, and complete them under their teacher's supervision. This approach maximizes student involvement, but it can be unwieldy and time-consuming. Learning may be uneven. Whole-group strategies work best when everyone's work is included, decisions are simple, and teachers wish to present basic ideas to the entire class.

A team approach offers another strategy. Here teachers organize the class into different groups, including one that acts as a curatorial team, consisting of just a few students. A small group can work efficiently yet retain enough autonomy for its members to learn their duties well. A curatorial team of three or four may also begin its work before its members' classmates become involved. It is a good idea to group students who have curated before with students who have less experience, so the "veterans" can help the "novices." In that way, the novices learn new curatorial skills, as the work progresses along smoothly. The curatorial-team members should work together as equal partners, while their teacher continues to oversee them. Eventually, the teacher and the curatorial team draw in other teams of designers, installers, publicists, and docents to work with them.

When employing a team strategy, teachers sometimes define basic parameters and objectives, such as team composition, thematic type, venue, installation style, time frame and budget, and the extent of the publicity, to facilitate the process. The specific theme and exhibition design are, of course, the responsibilities of the curators and the designers. Exigencies of time, money, and previous experience influence these decisions. Teachers may also decide on these parameters if they have planned an exhibition curriculum in which specific goals, concepts, and skills will be introduced in a certain sequence or time period.

TEAMWORK AND CONSENSUS BUILDING

Vision and leadership characterize an effective curatorial team. Through consensus-building, team members can develop a shared vision, and through teamwork, they can carry their intentions forward to others. The curators must learn to work together before they can expect to lead other teams involved in the exhibition. At first, they may have many ideas to discuss deliberately and respectfully. In the end, only one will emerge as the vision for the show.

By outlining rules for brainstorming and for examining ideas, teachers can set clear goals and help teams understand what is expected of them. When teams are asked to report back to their teacher with a list of all their ideas, along with pros and cons for each one, they will be able to articulate their needs and wishes more clearly and with greater conviction.

Ideas for exhibitions come from many sources. Works of art themselves often inspire shows. Students and their teachers know when they have done outstanding work that deserves recognition and praise. A body of work should prompt them to ask, "What is the essential, underlying idea that runs through all these paintings?" When students draw their ideas and themes from a given body of artwork, they are thinking inductively. They are synthesizing a common hypothesis from preexisting objects, experiences, and learning.

Sometimes an idea springs forth as little more than an intuition, a need to set forward a certain idea, or a desire to express a wonderful feeling. It may begin as a conversation, as an experience, or in response to a shared need. When the idea comes first and works of art then must be found or created to exemplify that idea, the approach is deductive. Evidence (works of art) that supports the hypothesis must be then gathered and scrutinized.

In either case, the initial idea must be transformed into a clear vision that the curators can rally around if they expect to convince other exhibition teams of its merit and, ultimately, to influence the public with their point of view. Their idea, their vision, needs to be clearly stated as a theme. Within an art exhibition, a theme is regarded as an important idea that is intended to influence viewers in a positive way. This definition of a theme, and by extension, of an exhibition, should be taught early and often. By always expecting themes to be important ideas that are meant to influence people in positive ways, teachers can deal constructively with assertions that may arise from trivial, poorly crafted, ill-conceived, or offensive art. Artwork, simply by virtue of being hung on a wall, does not necessarily reflect an important idea; nor can art intended to shock hope to influence people in a positive way.

Curators intentionally try to articulate shared meanings that exist within works of art by arranging them in distinctive ways and promote relationships with their audience through the sequence in which they will be viewed. They almost always try to show them as positive, constructive, aesthetically pleasing, and meaningful. As Weisman and Hanes (1999) point out, "A theme explores human experience from a point of view and often can raise issues" (p. 1). Those devising exhibition themes therefore consider the audiences' points of view and how they will interpret and appreciate what they see.

Arthur Danto (1998) notes, "An exhibition [is] a combination of art works that support an idea" (p. 92). A theme expresses the essential idea of the exhibition in a single phrase or sentence, but it is not an absolute definition. Curators agree upon a theme through discussion, prudent decision making, and a search for consensus. To achieve consensus, each team member must feel that he or she has been heard and understood by the rest of the team, must be able to live with the decision or solution, and must be willing to commit to his or her role in carrying out the decision or implementing the solution (Harrington-Macklin, 1994).

The following scenario provides our first look as a middle school art class mounts an exhibition of student work. This episode shows how a four-student curatorial team developed a consensus around a theme.

> Mrs. Bailey chose four students, Gabrielle, Molly, Ali, and Donald, to be the curators for the next art exhibition at their middle school. Gabrielle and Molly had curated before; Ali and Donald had not. Mrs. Bailey decided that the content of the show would be chosen from their recent unit on ink drawings and visual symbols. The class had studied Albrecht Dürer's 1514 etching *Melencolia I* as their cultural reference. They began by reviewing what they had learned about Dürer's etching and his visual symbols. The unit had "clicked"

with Gabrielle and Ali; they felt they really understood how artists could explore their intuition and discover new meanings. Molly and Donald had been more interested in the discursive aspects of the print and how it could convey secret messages to other people.

"I think we should pick drawings that really show what the person was thinking," Donald said.

"How will the people looking at it know what the message really is?" asked Ali.

"I think some of our drawings are just good drawings. You know, good pictures," Donald piped in. "We should pick good drawings and not worry about what people think."

"But what kind of theme is that?" offered Gabrielle, reminding her fellow curators of their task.

"How can we make people understand there is more there than just what they see?" Ali persisted.

"All of our drawings have secret symbols in them," Molly responded. "That was the point of the unit: We had to create our own symbols but not make them so obvious that their meaning would be 'telegraphed,' like Mrs. Bailey said."

Gabrielle queried, "Well, are symbols and meanings the same thing?"

The four curators debated that point for several minutes and decided meanings are what you really think, while symbols are what you talk about—the names or images of ideas. "Symbols are pictures of meanings," Molly pointed out.

Ali exclaimed, "We drew meanings! What we drew had meanings, but they aren't spelled out. You have to figure them out, like a puzzle. How about 'Meanings are mysteries'!"

After some further discussion, the four curators agreed on a theme: "Hidden Meanings."

CATEGORIES OF THEMES

Themes crystallize ideas into a common goal toward which all the exhibition's diverse efforts can be directed. They define a clear objective that guides the breadth and depth of the research related to the exhibition. Once a theme has been decided on, the curators can determine with confidence which works of art will best represent it. Without a theme, the idea may never become clear and their efforts may remain spurious or superficial.

Realizing that themes fall into various categories according to underlying motives greatly helps teachers to guide students in selecting a theme for their exhibition. Six categories in which themes may be grouped are offered here:

- *Descriptive*: Interpret an idea or perception
- *Didactic*: Convey information or tell a story
- *Metaphorical*: Explore a symbolic relationship
- *Emotive*: Evoke a feeling
- *Honorific*: Praise an artist
- *Issue Oriented*: Express an opinion

Descriptive Themes: Interpret an Idea or Perception

The intent of a descriptive presentation of art is straightforward—to explain or interpret something that has been directly experienced. Descriptive art exhibitions focus on the conceptual content (idea) or visual subject matter of the artwork. The meaning comes from the artist/students' perceptions and learning—"Viewers will know what we learned about spiders after looking at our paintings of them." Young children may simply wish to show what they have created. Their teacher can encourage them to push beyond this initial impulse by suggesting that people who see their art will want to know more about it: "If you could tell people about your art, what would you say?"

Explaining does not mean that the art is incomplete or unclear. Young children, in particular, are quite self-assured about their art—it is exactly what it is. An explanation may result in how the work is arranged. If beauty is the goal, will placing certain works next to each other work best? What is being explained by the art itself?

Interpreting art approaches the problem slightly differently. Here the art suggests a second level of understanding, beyond simple description. The art represents another layer of meaning symbolically. Perhaps it shows what the artists were thinking or feeling; perhaps it signifies a meaning that is not depicted by the image as such.

Descriptive exhibition themes work well when the content is direct or needs to be interpreted directly. For example, art based on interdisciplinary learning (which may be complex) may benefit from a straightforward, descriptive presentation. Utilitarian art whose function is obvious may also lend itself to descriptive exhibitions.

The students at the Ross School in East Hampton, New York, under the tutelage of their art teachers, Jennifer Cross and Nichelle Wilson-Pickett, regularly develop exhibitions based on descriptive themes. For an example, see Figure 1.1 and Case 1.1 in Part II.

Didactic Themes: Convey Information or Tell a Story

Many art exhibitions are instructional, or didactic, in nature. Teachers routinely teach using themes that focus on important ideas in the curriculum or topics of special interest to students and that provide a means by which stu-

Figure 1.1. *Portraits* exhibition, the Ross School, East Hampton, New York. With the guidance of their teacher, Jennifer Cross, seventh-grade students curated a show of professional artists.

Photo: The Ross School

dents may express their own points of view. Sequencing is an important feature of instruction. The message of a demonstration, for example, can be effectively conveyed only if each bit of information is presented in its proper order.

The metaphor permeating this exhibition type is time. Time flows in only one direction, with causes leading to effects. The didactic format brings together individual works of art by sequencing them in a temporal fashion, from beginning to middle to end. In many museum exhibitions of individual artists or of groups of artists, works of art are organized in a chronological or historical fashion, beginning with early works or influential precedents, advancing through various stages of development and maturing complexity, and arriving finally at a summative, grand finale. This organizes the events and accomplishments of an artist's life, a time period, or a style clearly and conveniently. Retrospectives often assume this format. Most people immediately recognize the underlying cognitive framework and readily accommodate to it.

Children overflow with stories they want to tell. The notion that an art exhibition can illustrate a story makes perfect sense to them. Like all narrative contexts, narrative art exhibitions tell stories. Younger children can often summarize an entire story in one picture, recounting a shared tale in a montage of vignettes with each capturing its own distinct point of view. As they grow older, each child might choose to concentrate on a specific scene in the story that has special significance for him or her. In these instances, the various works of art need to be organized sequentially from beginning to end for the story to be narrated properly.

A narrative is a literary concept, and the elements of literature—description, characterization, conflict and resolution, and protagonist/antagonist, among others—offer themselves as visual concepts as well. Most students appreciate the work of illustrators and understand how they can create illustrations to visually depict various episodes in a story. Narratives also suggest a temporal parameter of beginning, middle, and end in which content must be laid out sequentially to depict a chronology or history. It may be noted here that multicultural themes lend themselves to historical narrative settings.

Jean Sousa and the curatorial staff at the Art Institute of Chicago worked with an "Art Team," a dozen elementary school children who served as an advisory group, during the design-development stage of the exhibition, which used a didactic theme. Case 1.2 in Part II describes their exhibition, *Telling Images: Stories in Art*, more fully.

Metaphorical Themes: Explore a Symbolic Relationship

Metaphors offer wonderful opportunities for themes. Arguably, themes are metaphors. They represent relationships that beg to be explored and developed visually. Works of art often allude to other things through imagery and symbols. Artists explore formal and symbolic relationships within each work of art as they create it, weaving metaphors together from many sources. When artists exhibit their work, these relationships multiply exponentially, because the potential relationships now extend between works of art as well as within each of them. The exhibition theme must synthesize all these relationships into a metaphor that can be reasonably grasped and appreciated.

Exhibitions provide limitless opportunities for exploring all the facets of metaphor and analogy. They raise the question of how the content in works of art functions and whether it can be stretched even further. Exhibitions help students come to terms with tricky aesthetic questions at their own level of understanding by asking them to construct appropriate metaphors that their viewing audience will readily understand.

Metaphors elaborate. Taken at face value, the metaphor "A city is a beehive" is not very interesting when repeated over and over again, even in the artwork of an entire class. The metaphor becomes richer when its various aspects—transportation, food, security, housing, care for the young—are explored through elaboration.

There are many kinds of metaphors. For instance, images pertain to specific objects, but allegories are images of people that refer to abstract ideas or values. Signs are broader tokens that suggest a type instead of a specific item. They possess enough features to be recognized as a particular kind but they are also abstract enough to be generalized. Symbols, even when they depict particular objects as representational images, refer to meanings, not to the specific objects they portray. At that point, the image becomes imagery. Symbols often operate together in a context that prompts the viewer to read them as symbols and prevents them from being misread as literal images or general signs.

As Stevie Mack (1999) noted, "Symbols have culturally significant meanings" (n.p.). At the cultural level, symbols often reside within myths that provide us with a fountainhead of themes. Archetypal themes pervade our visual culture and are endlessly repeated in every manner, from fairy tales to movie plots to consumer advertising. They are so ubiquitous, they need only be hinted at subliminally to elicit a response. By recalling these familiar yet elusive idylls, one conjures up metaphors that echo deeply within many people. Myths provide immediate contexts for metaphors.

Metaphors recognize a similarity between two dissimilar things; analogies compare similar relationships between dissimilar things. "The brain is a computer" is a metaphor that cites a functional similarity between a human organ and an electronic device, while "The brain is a computer as the heart is a pump" describes an analogy that extends that similarity to other organs and devices. Metaphors relate A to B, while analogies follow the model A is to B as C is to D.

Gibson (1961) cites four types of analogies: personal, symbolic, direct, and fantasy. Personal analogies project qualities we find in ourselves (how we think, feel, act) into that which we do not understand. Symbolic analogies, by contrast, force us to "think outside the box" by looking at the problem in an unusual way. Direct analogies compare similar structures directly; for example, an electronic communication network is seen as similar to the human neural system. Fantasy analogies allow the artist to dismiss reality by substituting fanciful "what-ifs." Gibson (1961) links fantasy analogies with Sigmund Freud's idea of wish fulfillment. He notes, "The wish-fulfillment theory reveals the connection between the artist's motives as a human being and his chosen method of gratifying them" (p. 49). Each of these strategies gives rise to new ways of thinking and seeing, just as do art exhibitions. Encouraging students to develop themes in these various ways adds greatly to the types of themes they can create as well as the variety of actual themes.

Art is rich with symbols, and the more versatile that students become in working with metaphorical content and contexts the better. Metaphorical themes enrich the quality of art exhibitions at every level.

Ruth Slotnick developed the metaphors of icons and altars with children in a series of exhibitions held at the New Art Center in Newtonville, Massachusetts. To read more about her exciting shows, go to Case 1.3 in Part II.

Emotive Themes: Express a Feeling

Many curators aim at eliciting a certain emotional response from their audiences by creating a specific mood that will evoke the desired feeling. In this case the curators must focus their theme on that emotion and create an overall ambience that evokes that mood. All the components of the exhibition—lighting, installation, and trappings, as well as the art itself—must be meshed together successfully to induce that certain ambience.

To young children especially, it makes sense that collectively their paintings of, for example, flowers can have a theme of joy or playfulness, and then actually elicit that emotion. Their painting lesson may have dealt with noticing forms or mixing colors, but the exhibition theme should extend their experience affectively. The transition from particular paintings to a shared theme flows naturally, because each child had expressive feelings while creating his or her painting. This shift from a lesson concept to an exhibition theme different from that concept is important, because it stretches how the students conceptualize the theme and the show.

As children mature, their feelings become more complex and sophisticated. The same creative project may evoke many different emotions or depths of feelings. If the students are well grounded in eliciting emotions in a type of exhibition, they can also sort through their emotions to find a suitable theme. Diana Giardi (Cross & Giardi, 2003b) asks her students to associate emotions with specific aspects of life: pain in relation to the loss of love, fear in relation to war, or anger in relation to confinement. She also requires them to clarify their intent in a written statement that explains what they are trying to accomplish or express in their art. This statement can take a creative form, such as poetry, prose, or a quotation, if the student desires.

Conversations about feelings and art lead to discussions about taste and beauty that, in turn, can lead to more formal aesthetic reflections. A significant step occurs when the students reach beyond their own emotional needs to exhibit and consider the viewer's point of view. At that point, the sympathetic emotion of the student-artists who have shared a common experience can become empathetic to others.

Students may feel that their emotionally charged works of art are sufficient to convey their feelings. However, creating an overall mood that permeates the exhibition's atmosphere will draw the viewer in more immediately and effectively. By thoughtfully considering how to construct a conducive climate that pervades the exhibition, students can greatly extend the impact of their artworks. Props, colors, lighting, installation design, the tenor of the publicity, and their own attitudes contribute to the ambience. The students' behavior at the opening of the exhibition can be a key element in the exhibition's atmosphere. They may decide what their own emotive state will be and rehearse how they might project it.

Emotive exhibitions are an extremely important type of exhibition. At some level, in most art exhibitions there is an attempt to elicit an emotional response. Too often, however, the curator (or the artist) does not understand this exhibition type sufficiently and may settle for a heavy-handed approach designed to shock or even evoke a negative reaction. Ideally, art exhibitions provide a constructive social benefit. Teachers need to emphasize how to artfully elicit the mood the students truly wish for in their art and the ambience they truly desire in their exhibitions. They themselves must become receptive and critical viewers.

Brenda Jones's students at Wichita High School East, in Wichita, Kansas, probed deeply inside themselves for an emotive theme that evolved into *Origins*, an exhibition they held at the Wichita Center for the Arts (Jones, 1993). They tell how they did it in Case 1.4, in Part II.

Honorific Themes: Praise an Artist

Everyone, especially students, loves praise. Honorific exhibitions focus more on the artist than on the art. Art exhibitions provide dozens of ways to lavish attention on students in groups or as individuals. The praise is especially effective when the students' ideas or visions are interpreted. This goes well beyond a perfunctory display of their artwork and shifts away from skill and talent as a basis for exhibition.

When the theme for an honorific exhibition gravitates around a famous artist who has inspired the students' art, it is called a theme of *homage*. An artist can pay homage to a revered predecessor, as Pablo Picasso did when he alluded to Francisco José de Goya's *Third of May, 1808* in his own painting *Guernica*. Sydney Walker's (2001) notion of "big ideas" describes the artistic and aesthetic motives pervading the work of professional artists. After studying a big idea, students are encouraged to pursue it in their own way in their own art. A key distinction here is that the students interpret the master artist's motives and ideas; they don't simply mimic styles or techniques in a pastiche or copy works literally. Big ideas provide excellent themes for art exhibitions, as long as they incorporate interpretations and avoid mimicry.

Commemorative exhibitions also fall into this category. They can honor student artists at a particular time, such as graduation. Commemorative exhibitions draw together representative works from the artist's career, as in a retrospective exhibition. Art exhibitions can commemorate events in a celebratory fashion as well. A winning football team may provoke exhilaration for the whole school and inspire a wonderful art lesson. It can just as easily inspire a lively art exhibition. Nonholiday occasions calling for celebration occur throughout the entire school year. Concerts, plays, PTA meetings, and other gatherings provide ideal opportunities, as well as themes, for exhibiting art. Annual school- and districtwide shows celebrate art with the whole community.

Each year, Jenn Eisenheim and April Rao's (2001) fifth graders mount a retrospective of their artwork, which they have been gathering since kindergarten. These exhibitions, which reflect and honor young artists as they move toward graduation from elementary school, are eagerly awaited each year in their town. How they do it is described in Case 1.5, in Part II.

Issue-Oriented Themes: Reflect an Opinion

Traditionally, art exhibitions raise awareness, inform minds, and influence opinions. Students are quite aware of society's many political, social, economic, and ecological problems, but they often feel frustrated because adults don't listen to their pleas. As a result, they may feel helpless to "do anything." Every social ill comprises a nexus of themes ripe for expression and exhibition, yet unraveling these complex issues requires considerable thought and insight.

Exhibiting art can provide a positive, constructive forum for students' anxieties, opinions, and expressions, while at the same time encouraging them to go beyond their immediate emotional reactions to develop a reasoned and reasonable commentary. Exhibiting art can be an effective way to take action toward a social cause, whether it is an attempt to influence reform, raise money, or simply focus attention. Angry people are not effective; effective people are not angry. The underlying premise of issue-oriented exhibitions must be "Keep it positive in order to effect change." If the students wish to sway viewers' opinions, they cannot alienate them; they must win them over.

Autumn Sears built upon the intense social consciousness of her students to create art that reflected their reactions to conflict in the world and to select an issue-oriented theme for their exhibition. Case 1.6 in Part II details how Sears developed that issue-oriented theme.

DEVELOPING CRITERIA FROM THEMES

The theme permeates every aspect of an exhibition, especially the art that makes up its content. To select works of art that best exemplify the theme, curators must develop appropriate criteria. Deriving criteria from themes is important and should be given the utmost attention by the curators, because the art making up an exhibition must reflect its theme. That is an essential goal of any exhibition. By selecting artwork using objective criteria, students will think more deeply about their theme, look more critically at the art before them, and act more fairly in making their choices. If they feel confident in their selections and can explain them if challenged, they will remain motivated and enthusiastic about the show. When their choices are subjective and capricious, both curators and artists may feel that the selections are arbitrary, impulsive, and unfair, and their enthusiasm may falter. A pervasive feeling that the exhibition is "built on sand" may creep in.

Criteria constitute clear descriptions that can be matched to the artistic, aesthetic, pictorial, or symbolic features of works of art. Criteria clarify and strengthen themes, which often must be modified when it is revealed that they are not totally feasible. In teacher terms, themes are to criteria as concepts are to objectives. They are the operational form of conceptual definitions or relationships.

Curators need to exercise teamwork in order to develop criteria that they can finally agree upon. Teamwork also allows them to select art that exemplifies their theme. The first step in developing solid criteria is to decide what the theme really means. Each of the thematic types has an underlying motive that serves as its dominant criteria. For example, issue-oriented themes seek to express an opinion and influence the viewer while metaphorical themes emphasize relationships. Other criteria such as craftsmanship and design may also play roles. Criteria change from theme to theme. Expression, for instance, may be desirable but not necessary in a descriptive exhibition; realistic likenesses may be impressive but not required for emotive art.

The scenario introduced earlier in the chapter continues with the curatorial team developing the criteria they will use to select the student drawings to be exhibited:

Gabrielle, Molly, Ali, and Donald had previously decided on a theme, "Hidden Meanings," for their exhibition of paintings based on a unit about visual symbols and Dürer's etching *Melencolia I*.

"If our show is going to be about hidden meanings," Gabrielle said, "then we have to figure out how to get people to realize that what they're looking at are really symbols.

"And," Donald continued, "how to look for the meanings and discover them."

"They should have symbols that can be figured out," Molly suggested, "but not really simple ones, like hearts or peace signs."

"I agree," Ali added. "The assignment was to create our own symbols for things that have real meaning for us. So the drawings should have both real meanings and real symbols."

"And they should be able to be decoded," Donald emphasized.

After sorting out their intentions a bit further, the curators had Molly, the recorder for the team, write down the first important criteria, "The drawing should have real symbols with significant meanings."

Donald pointed out that one important thing they had learned in this drawing unit was that symbols had to be decoded. They had all worked hard to find the right balance between symbols that were too obvious ("telegraphed," as Mrs. Bailey described them), and symbols that were so cryptic that they could never be figured out. "That should be another criteria; they should be able to be decoded," said Donald, and Molly added that as the second criteria.

Molly pointed out that Mrs. Bailey had emphasized how they arranged their symbols in their overall compositions as an important aspect of making visual symbols work. She said, "Composition definitely has to be a criteria because that's one way you know they are symbols in the first place, and besides, the symbols play off against one another." After some discussion, the group came up with another criteria: "The composition enhances the effect of the visual symbols."

Gabrielle noted that they had learned a lot about the technical aspects of drawing and craftsmanship in this unit. Mrs. Bailey had emphasized that over and over again. "Let's make craftsmanship another criteria," Gabrielle asked.

"How do you state that?" Ali wondered.

"Craftsmanship shows when you take the time to do a good job and care about what you're doing," Gabrielle answered. "It could be, 'The drawing shows technical skill and caring.'"

Armed with this list of criteria and the discussion that produced it, the curators were able to select the artwork that best represented the theme for their show.

Rubrics work well for developing effective thematic criteria. The curatorial team first makes a list of general categories to serve as criteria. Next, they write short descriptions for each of them. The descriptions in the *Satisfactory* column should be written first, because they provide the basis upon which other descriptions may be elaborated upon or shown to be lacking. For example, a *Satisfactory* description for the criterion, "Real symbols with significant meaning," might be "the drawing has several original symbols with personal meanings." From there, it is easy to imagine how some art might exceed that criterion. "The drawing has unique symbols that are integrated into an important, personal meaning" clearly, yet reasonably, excels beyond the *Satisfactory* level, while "The symbols are obvious, trite, or conventional" spells out why other art may fall short. The clearer the descriptions are in the minds of the curators, the easier it is to match artwork with them and to justify those decisions.

If Mrs. Bailey's students had chosen to develop criteria using a rubric format, it might have looked something like the example shown in Figure 1.2

SELECTING ART

Selecting art poses a controversial problem for exhibiting student art. Some educators believe that students may be traumatized if their work is not selected. This potential problem may be averted by selecting work following the exhibition theme and objective criteria and avoiding subjective decisions.

A problem may arise if some students' art is never selected. This can be avoided by having frequent shows throughout the school year, thus providing many opportunities for every student to exhibit. Teachers can ensure that all students will have their art shown regularly by keeping good records about who has and has not exhibited, rotating between groups (half will exhibit this week, half next week) and having "Teacher's Choice" shows periodically ("Mary, Sue, and Jim, I would like you to begin curating a show that includes your work").

The "artist of the week" format uses a rotation method to ensure that every child is eventually honored. Two children work with the artist of the

Figure 1.2. A Rubric for Selecting Artwork

Theme: "Hidden Meanings"	Excellent	Satisfactory	Needs work
Real symbols with significant meanings	The drawing has unique symbols that are integrated into a important, personal meaning	The drawing has several original symbols with personal meanings	The symbols are obvious, trite, or conventional
Decoding	The symbols have multiple layers of meaning but can be decoded with effort	The symbols are able to be decoded with minimal effort	The symbols "telegraph" their meanings
Composition	The symbols are strongly integrated into the composition to make a meaningful whole	The symbols are integrated into the composition satisfactorily	Weak composition; symbols are not integral parts of the composition
Craftsmanship	Obvious caring and skillful craftsmanship; a complex, detailed whole	Satisfactory caring and craftsmanship; a complete whole	Lacking in caring and craftsmanship; not integrated as a whole

week to display his or her work. The following week, one curator drops off the team and last week's artist becomes a curator for the next artist. This method works well in self-contained classrooms and where the school year allows enough weeks to present every young artist in the class. This exhibition strategy is arbitrary and should be used to supplement a regular exhibition schedule that ensures that every student has several occasions to show his or her work throughout the school year.

Multiple opportunities also should pertain to the various roles within the exhibition process. Eventually, everyone should have a chance to be a curator, a designer, an installer, a publicist, and a host or docent. Different venues and the scope and purpose of shows should provide more than enough opportunities to exhibit.

By carefully choosing various categories of themes—descriptive, didactic, metaphorical, emotive, honorific, and issue oriented—a wise teacher will underwrite a variety of cognitive strategies. A descriptive theme will elicit descriptive art; an emotive theme will draw out expressive art, and usually a different mix of children. The specific themes within each of these categories further elaborate the mix.

Basing exhibitions on themes and developing objective means for selecting art remains the best strategy for an effective selection process. When themes are clearly articulated and selections stem from objective criteria instead of subjective preferences, students remain confident in the process and in the shows.

Although some teachers, particularly in the lower grades, may prefer to exhibit all the art of a class, inevitably there comes a point when space, time, and effort require that only some art can be shown, while other works cannot. It is essential that the selection process be objective for the good of both the students and the exhibition. Moving students toward an objective selection strategy can be done incrementally over a flexible period of time. In what follows, I outline a series of steps that guides students gradually toward a more objective stance

1. All the students' work is exhibited. The students are mainly concerned with the arrangement of the art, often preferring to place their art next to a friend's.
2. The teacher saves several weeks' artwork, and the students select works from their own or a neighbor's portfolio. All the children are exhibited.
   - Each child chooses *one* of his or her own works, either through personal preference or based on a broad theme.
   - Working as partners, two children select *one* work from each of their two portfolios. The pair should discuss which works they selected and why.

- Students trade portfolios with one another and choose one work based on a shared theme. Each child may write or speak about the reason for their selection.

3. The teacher announces that all the work will not fit in the exhibition area, such as a bulletin board, and suggests that half the work will be displayed this week, and half next week. The children select which art will be exhibited each week and offer reasons for their selections.

4. The students list several possible themes for a show but can't decide which one to use. The teacher suggests that they choose two and divide the art between the two themes. All the art will be shown, but in two different locations. The students make their selections based on the two themes, giving reasons for their choices.

5. The teacher points out that the students have already had shows with didactic, emotive, and descriptive themes. She mentions that the artwork suggests an issue-oriented theme (which narrows the thematic perspective somewhat). The students develop appropriate criteria for an issue-oriented theme.

6. The space for a show allows only a limited number of works. Using criteria developed from their theme, the students select an appropriate number of works. Only a few students are exhibited. This strategy can be used again with different artworks until all the students have shown their work.

7. As students become aware of various installation designs, they will come to understand that exhibition designs influence the number of works that can be hung. For example, salon-style installations crowd many works of art together in a space while linear installation designs call for just a few works of art spaced relatively far apart.

This sequence of selection strategies may take several months to present. However, it gradually builds confidence in the exhibition process; allays anxieties about being exhibited, or not; emphasizes the importance of themes; and shifts the criteria for selection progressively toward objective, rather than subjective, bases. It also allows teachers to reiterate many times the three fundamental principles that underlie all exhibitions:

- Exhibitions should be thoughtful and deliberate in order to inform people about the art itself and the ideas contained in it. Hence, the central importance of themes.
- Exhibitions should be visually attractive in order to attract and hold attention. Hence, the importance of good design and installation.
- Other people will view the exhibition. Therefore, exhibitions should strive toward a social purpose in order to influence viewers' opinions in a positive way. Hence, the importance of attending to the social

perspective of the viewing public as well as the social dynamics of the teams mounting the exhibition itself.

When teachers emphasize these principles early and often, the quality and value of exhibiting grows steadily.

Saving several weeks' work can pose storage problems. Making certain that the works are small and flat minimizes the problem; varying the media and subjects boosts interest. Each of these instructional strategies may be used several times until the students are comfortable and confident with them. By being attentive to students' needs and expectations, the teacher will know how long to remain at a certain level and when to move on. Eventually, these selection strategies can be taken over by teams of curators.

Michele Dangelo worked with third-grade students at Orleans Elementary School in Orleans, Massachusetts, to curate a show from the collection at the Cape Museum of Fine Arts, in Dennis. In Case 1.7, in Part II, she describes how she prepared the students to view, research, and finally select the works they wanted.

Let's return to the scenario of Mrs. Bailey's class as the curators select the drawings to be exhibited:

> Given the size of the drawings and how much space they had to display them, Gabrielle, Molly, Ali, and Donald knew they could only select 18 out of 29 drawings for their show. Mrs. Bailey had taught her students to look at each work of art according to the criteria they had written. Viewing each drawing in turn, they decided which of the four criteria was represented most strongly and most weakly in each work. These two elements permitted them to go through the artwork quickly yet prompted discussion about most of the works. As they went through the drawings to winnow out a number of them, they discovered that some touched on more criteria than did others. Within a short time they had found 18 that satisfied most of their criteria and the theme.

CONCLUSION

"Since collections can be arranged in countless different ways," Belcher (1991) observes, "the selection of appropriate themes is a fundamental issue which needs to be resolved" (p. 16). Themes are the backbone of art exhibitions. They distinguish worthwhile exhibitions from simplistic displays. Themes infuse each exhibition with a unique meaning and ultimately guide its design, "look," and presentation. The theme, or idea, needs to be broad enough to embrace all the works included in the exhibition, yet specific enough to clearly express its own distinctive focus.

The themes found in the case studies related to this chapter each have specific subjects or slogans for exhibitions. However, it is the broad categories underlying them that are intended to encourage teachers and curators to think beyond conventional limits and strive toward new horizons. Many exhibitions are descriptive or didactic, but they could easily be metaphorical, emotive, honorific, issue oriented, or fantastic. Stretch your imagination!

Exhibitions often cover a particular culture, period of history, style, artist, or medium. Yet it would be simplistic, if not misleading, to fall into a "cultural" or "historical" theme. Cultures, history, styles, and other aspects of art can all be cast in descriptive, didactic, metaphorical, emotive, honorific, or issue-oriented exhibition themes. The content of art should not be confused with the intent of an exhibition theme.

Themes are the core ideas of exhibitions. They provide the clear, shared vision around which all planning and presentation is built. Consequently, developing an adequate theme is essential for a successful exhibition as well as successful learning.

Selecting art is one of the most problematic aspects of exhibition. The chosen works should exemplify the theme fully. Yet social factors and individual feelings need to be considered. By making the selection process as objective as possible, and by ensuring that each student will have many opportunities to exhibit throughout the school year, these potential problems can be prevented. Developing clear criteria upon which to base choices works well. Further clarifying the criteria with written descriptors in a rubric framework helps even more.

Once everyone shares a thematic vision of the show's intention, students can go ahead with hanging a small, immediate show. Bigger exhibits require a longer time frame and more thorough design planning before installation.

CHAPTER 2

Exhibition Design

For several centuries, the accepted method for displaying art in museums, galleries, and homes was the salon style, in which works of art crowded one another from wainscot to ceiling. Gilt-framed paintings ostentatiously decorated every inch of wall surface to exhibit wealth and prestige as much as taste and beauty. Gradually, ideas about art changed, and how art was exhibited changed as well.

The period from 1900 to 1938, just prior to World War II, was an era of exuberant experimentation in exhibiting, especially in Europe. Many artists strove to be avant-garde, each new art movement winning recognition for itself by outdoing its competitors with still more radical art and even more outrageous shows. Fauvism, Cubism, Surrealism, Futurism, and Dadaism galvanized public attention as much through the artists' exhibition antics as through their art. Working outside major museums and established galleries in many cases, artists mounted their own exhibitions to announce their new aesthetic epiphanies.

> The difference in [the International Exposition of Surrealism, held at the Galerie Beaux-Arts, in Paris, in 1938] was the physical setting, installations that clearly overwhelmed the works shown within them. This constituted the show's unique aspect, turning the exhibition itself into a work of art on a par with its content. To an extent this was true of the Berlin Dada Fair [of 1920], the chaotic and aggressive presentation expressing the same message as the pieces presented. But at the Galerie Beaux-Arts the intention was more explicit, the installation designed to evoke the disquiet of repressed desire on the verge of self-recognition, the viewer placed in a world displaying its own Surrealist interpretation. (Altshuler, 1994, p. 133)

Even commercial exhibitions intended to showcase industry's new products broke away from staid, formal displays. Lilly Reich's innovations in her career as an exhibition designer in Germany during the 1920s and 1930s paralleled the attention-grabbing bravado of the prewar avant-garde artists. She was one of the few designers to present raw materials and technical processes rather than finished products as the substance of her exhibitions. Luxurious velvets and silks hanging from ceiling to floor sinuously meandered through the café of the 1927 *Women's Fashion Show* in Berlin. Massive, rough-hewn logs represented a furniture manufacturer at the 1931 *Materials Show*. Sensuous materials compelled visitors to experience rather than to simply look (McQuaid, 1996).

During the 1920s, formalist ideas in art began to influence how art was shown. Excessive clutter and opulent wall hangings gave way to a more austere look. By the 1940s, following modernist precepts of simplicity and clarity, Alfred Barr Jr., the curator of the Museum of Modern Art in New York, and others popularized another installation style, which featured just a few superlative works rather than walls being completely covered (Staniszewski, 1998). Works of art in plain frames were hung at eye level on neutral backgrounds and widely spaced one from another, so only one work of art filled the viewer's field of vision at a time. With this minimalization of peripheral distractions viewers could concentrate on each work individually. This type of installation became known, somewhat sarcastically, as the "white cube" style, after the antiseptic white walls and harsh, clinical lighting. It continues to prevail today in contemporary galleries and museums, where gallery visitors (and many installation designers) take it for granted. While the white cube offers a visually pristine presentation for art, other installation designs offer visually stimulating and intellectually imaginative alternatives.

DESIGNING AN EXHIBITION

For designers, an exhibition represents a unique opportunity to experience art in a certain time and space. The experience is, of course, visual, but it also can become emotional, social, political, and intellectual. To a large extent, designers must plan (or at least, anticipate) *how* the viewers will see the art by arranging it in a specific way within a certain space. Carter, DeMao, and Wheeler (2000) observe that designing an exhibition "begins with a story one wishes to tell, a lesson one hopes to demonstrate, a collection of objects or artifacts one must display. Exhibition design involves the process of finding appropriate form and authentic expression and content" (pp. 8–10).

Time plays the most significant, yet least appreciated, role. Exhibition designers must plan how the viewers' experience of the art will unfold:

- Will they mill about, viewing works in no particular order and randomly make their own aesthetic connections?
- Will they be guided along a prescribed path with a definite beginning, middle, and end?
- Will people pass by the art in two directions, as in a school hall?
- Will they view the art passively or engage it interactively?

Exhibition designers aim at creating a satisfying encounter between viewers and art. How the viewers will interpret what they see requires as much consideration as the works of art themselves. The works must be arranged so they complement one another attractively, but they must also hold the viewers' attention intellectually and emotionally. McAlpine and Giangrande (1998) point out, "Putting a collection together is about setting a scene and creating an atmosphere. . . . The strength of a group or a solitary object should engage the eye and arouse the senses, not just because of the objects themselves but because of the way in which they are arranged" (p. 128).

When youngsters first start exhibiting, their sense of exhibition design may be influenced by a desire to place their work next to that of their friends or have it in the "best" place. They may arbitrarily hang the first work in the upper left of the wall and proceed piece by piece to the right in a manner reminiscent of that of reading and writing. These spontaneous installations can be quite charming and inventive. However, unless they are guided by a theme, they may revert to simplistic decoration instead of producing a thoughtfully conceived exhibition. A theme infuses all the works of art with a unique visual and spatial arrangement. It orchestrates individual works of art into a whole that maximizes their novel features and strengths while forging relationships between the various works.

During the initial phase, the student-curators conceive a theme with respect to a certain body of artworks. When designing the exhibition, another perspective, that of the viewers, provides an advantageous starting point. The students composing the design team need to consider how viewers will interact with the exhibition as a whole and the works of art within it. The whole exhibition should carry out its underlying theme in the most effective manner possible.

Like the other phases of creating an exhibition, designing an installation can and should be a team effort. Sometimes the curatorial team extends their duties into this next phase because they grasp the theme best. Ideally, other students should be drawn into the enterprise at this point, so more of them can participate in the exhibition process as early as possible.

One alternative is to assign each of the student-curators to lead one of the other teams. In this way, the design, installation, publicity, and event teams can function independently and efficiently yet proceed together on the same timetable. As members of the various teams, the curators can reiterate the theme and guide their peers toward a coordinated outcome. The curators will probably continue to meet periodically to check progress, discuss problems, and update decisions.

The key is communication. The members of the curatorial team must clearly convey their thematic vision to other students to a degree that they understand what is required and are motivated to work toward the stated

goal. In this way, the curators gain cooperation from their peers. Cooperation leads to coordination between the various teams, which, in turn leads
to a successful exhibition.

The following scenario introduces the design team in Mrs. Bailey's art class:

Gabrielle had worked with three other students on the curatorial
team to develop a theme for their ink drawings inspired by Dürer's
Melencolia I. Because of the symbolic content of their drawings, the
student-curators had decided on a metaphorical theme, "Hidden
Meanings," which was intended to draw attention to the cryptic
elements within their drawings.

Mrs. Bailey assigned Gabrielle to lead the design team. Its exhibition would be in the high school's main lobby. One side of the open
area was a glass wall adjacent to the entrance, and the opposite side
presented large, flat walls that were ideal for two-dimensional work.
There was steady traffic through this area during the day, but not the
rushing hoards that crowded the halls each time classes changed.

Gabrielle explained the idea of "Hidden Meanings" to Nadi,
Jamal and Rachel, the other members of her design team. As she
pointed out, metaphorical themes explore symbolic relationships,
which made it a logical choice for their symbolic drawings. They
spread out the 18 drawings selected by the curators to look at them
as a group.

Jamal said, "If we use some standing panels near the windows,
we'll have enough room to display each piece separately. Then they
can get in close and really look at them." (Jamal was thinking of a
linear installation design, in which each work has its own space.)

"That's a good idea," Rachel replied, "but I think it's too simple.
I mean, we really worked hard on these drawings. We know what
they mean; we know how the symbols work, but other people won't.
They'll see a flower and nothing more. We should make them see the
symbols. Look at these four drawings. They all have plants or flowers
in them. If we hang them together, and write a note next to them
about how plants can be symbols, then they'll get it." (Rachel was
alluding to a synoptic installation design, in which works are grouped
by some shared similarity.)

Nadi piped up, "I like the idea of comparing the drawings, but
remember, Mrs. Bailey said that our symbols had to have real meanings but they shouldn't be really obvious. She said not to 'telegraph' the
meanings. If we could make people really look at the drawings but still
have to figure them out, that would be cool." (Nadi was referring to a
comparative installation design, in which paired works highlight their
own features through contrast with a complementary work.)

The group agreed that that was a great idea. Gabrielle asked if they thought a comparative installation fit the theme, and they decided it did.

The spatial placement of each work of art is critical in art exhibitions. For young children, simple spatial concepts such as right and left, above and below, horizontal, vertical, diagonal, and parallel are new ideas, and installations of art give concrete structure to these orientations. Ordinal sequences (first, second, third) present other new concepts. The fact that the artworks may be arranged in any number of ways poses endless intriguing opportunities. Arthur Danto (1998) points out that just 10 works of art can be arranged in more than 3 million different combinations. Luckily, just a few combinations prevail in our visual experience, and they form the basic strategies for exhibition installation design.

Some thematic types readily lend themselves to certain installation formats, and vice versa. For example, when designing an installation for a narrative or chronological theme, designers may find arranging the works sequentially to be quite logical and effective. However, any of the thematic types described in Chapter 1 can be used with any of the exhibition designs. It all depends on what viewing experiences the exhibition designers wish their audiences to have. Like thematic types, different installation designs, as described below, need to be tried out over an extended period of time in order for one to understand the possibilities and experience the alternatives.

INSTALLATION DESIGNS

In the following sections I describe six installation styles. The salon style is by far the most frequently used installation design in elementary schools. Linear installations are frequently employed in secondary schools where a more professional, "gallery" format is desired. Salon and linear styles are typical and traditional, but if overused, they can become hackneyed and clichéd. Teachers need to introduce new methods for exhibiting art, just as they continue to teach new ways of making art. Students should become acquainted with a variety of installation designs so they can come to recognize that physically arranging art in different ways can actually change how it is experienced, appreciated, and understood.

Salon-Style Design: A Sea of Art

Children's art is typically displayed in a salon fashion, with the maximum number of works closely nestled next to, above, and below one another. The diversity or quantity of the work; the desire to include the art of all students;

and limitations of time, space, and resources often compel these densely compacted arrays. However, salon installations can suffer if they lack a coherent, underlying theme. When works are thoughtfully assembled into a unifying pattern related to the work itself, they can truly become a whole that is greater than the sum of its parts. As the collector Charles Paget Wade pointed out, "A room can be filled with innumerable things and have a perfect sense of repose, if they are chosen with thought and care so as to form one harmonious background" (quoted in McAlpine & Giangrande, 1998, p. 46). Small works, in particular, can be clustered together for greater effect. Salon-style exhibitions require broadly conceived themes that can encompass many styles, expressions, or media.

Strongly patterned art can often be joined together very effectively. Geometric designs, for example, can be seamed into one large "quilt" to create a marvelous effect. When works are arranged at seemingly random angles, an overall sense of whimsy and playfulness prevails. Brightly colored mattes add to the fun.

Teachers often employ a salon-style installation for end-of-school-year shows, districtwide shows, and art festivals, where showing the work of every child is important.

Vikki Chenette worked with 10 other elementary art teachers in Natrona County School District in Casper, Wyoming, to produce a monthlong exhibit of their students' artwork. Case 2.1, describing her exhibition strategy, can be found in Part II.

Linear Design: Clear and Straightforward

As mentioned previously, linear design developed early in the 20th century, following Barr's desire to align works of art along an imaginary horizontal line located at eye level and to space them quite widely apart. However, because the meanings of the works are intended to be contemplated one work at a time, their arrangement often becomes arbitrary. Selections may be hung next to each other simply for reasons of overall formal design, such as balance (alternating large and small works) or color harmony (avoiding clashing colors). Consequently, one unintended side effect of linear design is that it offers little incentive to make visual or cognitive connections between various works of art. In a postmodern art scene, such connections are important, and other installation designs should be considered.

Linear design lends itself nicely to an eclectic body of artwork. When students have chosen works from a wide variety of media and subjects, this installation design works well.

Sherrie Sikora teaches art at Lincoln Middle School in La Crosse, Wisconsin. With the help of her students, she mounts six shows each year in a gallery within her school. The gallery is long and narrow, measuring 8 feet by 24 feet, which lends itself best to serial traffic patterns and linear exhibition designs. Case 2.2 in Part II tells about her use of linear design in her gallery.

Sequential Design: Successive and Progressive

A sequential design leads the viewer through the exhibition in a predetermined, step-by-step manner. Anyone who has taken an audio tour in a museum has had a sequential experience, no matter how the exhibition was installed. Many people prefer these prescribed tours. A sequential installation conducts the viewers along a predetermined labyrinth; visitors must enter at the beginning, trace through the exhibition according to a serial route, and exit at the end. There is a definite one-way flow. Bass emphasized sequential progression in *The Educationally Interpretative Exhibition* (1997) to the extent of attaching string to the works, to connect one to another, and between an artwork and its supporting text.

In literature, at the beginning of the story, characters are introduced, backgrounds described, and plots hatched. In the body of the story, questions are raised, schemes developed, and details elaborated on. Eventually, at the end, the conflicts are resolved and all the loose ends are tied up. When the students' art illustrates scenes from a story, they will find it fairly easy to arrange works by simply matching the narrative of the story. Sequential installations that develop from a beginning, through a middle, and to an end are "successive," each work logically following the one that preceded it.

Sequential designs can unfold in a progressive manner as well, each work building upon the work that preceded it and informing the work that follows it. In this case, the design culminates in a big finale. A series of works that show various stages of development illustrate progressive installation well. Also, when students create a collective piece, their creative and artistic progress leading up to the final, spectacular work provides a vivid and satisfying installation.

Jennifer Cross and her students at the Ross School, East Hampton, New York, used a sequential installation design that is described in Case 2.3 in Part II and shown in Figure 2.1.

Comparative Design: Juxtapositions That Contrast and Connect

Comparative designs place works (or groups of works) next to one another in combinations that invite visual comparisons or cognitive dissonances. Contrasting colors, for example, may play upon the viewers' perceptions. When the comparison is obvious, the perception is heightened and pleasant, and the connection is clear.

Figure 2.1. *Drawn from Nature*, the Ross School, East Hampton, New York. Jennifer Cross's students combined their studies in science and other subjects with art to produce a wide variety of observations, interpretations, and expressions related to nature.

Photo: The Ross School

When the connection between the contrasting works requires the viewers to think or question more deeply, tension builds. The viewers try to resolve the dilemma posed by the works, and that takes time and thought. Tension is provocative, and it may require heightened consciousness (at a cognitive level), empathy (at an emotional level), or conscience (at an ethical level) for viewers to resolve.

Diane Bingham (1994) discusses her approach when groups of children tour the J. P. Getty Museum, in Malibu, California, where she works:

> We teach with a limited number of carefully selected objects during the lesson rather than offering a tour of the entire museum. . . . At each stop we may focus on one object or perhaps do an activity that involves a comparison of several objects in one gallery. We want to demonstrate that it takes time to see the work of art, and that extended engagement with one object can be fun and rewarding. . . . When learning concepts, students need to connect the concept with something already in their experience; the more connections, the deeper will be their understanding. (p. 1)

The underlying structure of comparative juxtapositions is dualism. For every wrong, there is a right; for every light, there is dark. By matching highs with lows, both may be emphasized and made more poignant.

Rhythm creates a sensuous, emotional type of comparative installation by interspersing works that excite with their dramatic impact with those that refresh with their calmness. What constitutes intensity and tranquillity may be determined by the formal qualities of the works themselves, such as color and form, their styles, the moods they evoke, or their subject matter.

Rhythm appeals to the emotions. When the artworks vary considerably, or when they evoke emotional responses, rhythmic installation designs work well. They are also successful when the exhibition intends to capture a certain atmosphere or affective climate. The undulating rhythm may create a "call and response," in which the issues raised by one group of works are resolved by the next.

The watchword for rhythmic designs is *elaboration.* The design should develop in its complexity by elaborating upon the chosen theme at one or more points in the exhibition. Although the ebb and flow repeats, it should not be completely even. Perhaps the exhibition begins with a dramatic "overture," and evolves through several variations, before culminating in an impressive "crescendo."

One word of warning: The rhythm should not be between strong and weak works of art. This would very likely contradict whatever theme was being presented, as well as create a rather obvious pattern. One way to dramatize a group of works is to concentrate several works together, while physically spacing a few others farther apart to achieve a calming effect. In this way, strong and weak works can be mixed together at empathetic points.

Comparisons must be delicately balanced. There must be some connection between the juxtaposed works. It need not be obvious at first but the viewers should be able to resolve it eventually. If no connection is made, the viewers will just wander away muttering, "I don't get it." Then, neither the art nor its installation will be appreciated.

Peg Koetsch and the fourth-graders at Bailey's Elementary School of the Arts and Sciences in Falls Church, Virginia, created a comparative installation for their historical art exhibition. Case 2.4, in Part II, tells how they went about it.

Synoptic Design: Grouping by Similarities

When the body of artwork is large or diverse, a synoptic exhibition design may offer the perfect solution. A synoptic installation groups works of art into clusters that share some common trait: An exhibition of animal paintings may gather the mammals in one group, amphibians in another group, and birds in yet another group. Each group is a "synopsis," or brief summary, of a specific subject within a larger, more comprehensive context. The themes for synoptic groupings are many: medium, subject matter, artistic styles, grade level of the artists, and so forth. Each synoptic group shares similarities of one sort or another.

Episodic designs represent a variation of synoptic designs. Where synoptic groupings concentrate on distinguishable visual features of the artworks, episodes emphasize events or situations depicted in the works. Therefore, all the works related to a specific incident can form a separate episodic cluster.

While synoptic and episodic installations bring immediate order to an exhibition, it should not appear arbitrary. The groupings should be interesting enough to stand on their own and make their own thematic points. Concentrating similar works of art can emphasize their common features; revealing their shared qualities can make them more appealing.

Margaret Wood and her advanced art students at L. C. Bird High School in Chesterfield, Virginia, borrowed vintage photographs from the Virginia Museum of Fine Arts. They designed a synoptic installation with antiques and heirlooms for the first show in their school's new art gallery. Case 2.5 in Part II describes their synoptic installation.

Contextual Installation Design: Setting the Scene

A contextual design creates a setting in which works of art seem to fit naturally. Exhibits in ethnographic or natural history museums often employ this strategy. Cutaway huts provide an appropriate setting for native artifacts; dioramas create natural environments for taxidermy displays, and Egyptian tombs give a mysterious authenticity to mummies and grave treasures. Student art that has been inspired by traditional cultures can be carried to a more integrative and reflective level by developing a suitable context to house them. It doesn't take much: A layer of sand can suggest a natural setting; crumpled kraft paper can imply a prehistoric cave site.

Simple objects can complement the students' art and installation. Old books, furniture, and architectural settings provide clues and cues to the art's meaning. For instance, a background of maps, travel schedules, and old plane tickets might elaborate a theme of travel while the students' art depicts their adventures away from home. Artifacts from other cultures reiterate art based on those cultures.

Contexts can also be fanciful. A restaurant setting with tables, chairs, table linen, china, and flatware gives trompe l'oeil ceramic food an extra, imaginative push. Student-made jewelry can be attractively displayed in a jewelry-store vitrine or modeled on mannequins.

Case 2.6 in Part II describes how Robert Sabol and his students created complex contextual installations of art for their school in Crawfordsville, Indiana. See Figure 2.2 for an example of an African art installation.

Figure 2.2. African Art, the Children's Art Gallery. Crawfordsville, Indiana. Robert Sabol and his students developed a variety of exhibitions of their own work and works borrowed from museums and other sources.

Photo: Robert Sabol

DEVELOPING AN EXHIBITION BRIEF

During the planning phases, once students decide on their theme, they should draft an exhibition brief. An exhibition brief embodies a clear plan of action for an exhibition and is essential for any endeavor that takes more than a class period to organize. Curators should consult with other exhibition teams, but they usually oversee drafting the brief and approve its final form. For smaller shows, the entire class may assume this role or teachers may perform it themselves.

A brief specifies each step of the exhibition process and details in sequence all the assignments, tasks, and duties for each committee, team, and individual. Committees or teams can be small, but they should include at least one person with experience related to the particular task. Teams can be assembled by students' choosing among themselves, by scheduled rotation, or by assignment from the teacher. In the course of a school year, each student should serve on different teams and learn different skills. Some students who have been successful in one role may feel comfortable and try to remain in that role. In this respect, the teacher needs to maintain records of who has served on which teams and assign students to new teams so they can learn new skills.

Within the overall plan outlined in the brief, each team can decide, discuss, and determine its own tasks and duties. Students are more likely to understand their jobs and do them well if they plan them for themselves rather than being dictated to. Moreover, to develop various skills, students must grapple directly with the actual tasks themselves. As each team formalizes its own plans, it can bring them together, discuss them, and firm up any weak areas. The whole brief should be examined in relation to the theme—does the brief for this exhibition fulfill the theme we intended?

Even a simple exhibition benefits from having a brief, because it clarifies duties and helps each student know what he or she needs to do and when. As exhibitions become more complex, with teams and committees working independently yet striving to coordinate all their efforts, a brief becomes indispensable. Drafting a brief helps groups organize their planning, predict how much time they will need, arrange for resources they must gather and prepare, anticipate problems they might encounter, and above all, hone their social skills. Gradually extending their planning framework is one of the most valuable lessons students can learn. They become more reasonable in the expectations, more confident in their abilities, and more responsible in following through on their obligations, as shown in the continuing scenario:

> The curatorial committee for "Hidden Meanings," made up of Gabrielle, Molly, Kelly, and Donald, met with one representative of each of the other teams, to draft a brief and timetable for their show. Nadi represented the design team; Kendra, the installation team; Ward, the publicity team; and Timeka, the reception team. Each of the curators would serve on one of the other teams to maintain continuity with the theme. The curators explained the theme and its intent. Molly pointed out that their drawings all contained secret symbols that each artist had invented. The curators wanted to bring this feature out, but as Mrs. Bailey had said, not telegraph it by making the meanings obvious. Everyone asked questions.
>
> Mrs. Bailey gave them a date for the opening reception three weeks ahead. Nadi, Kendra, Ward, and Timeka volunteered their teams for specific duties and estimated when they would be done with each of them. Nadi said her team could have a design for the exhibition within a week, and they would show it to the curators at that time. Kendra said her installation group could have the individual labels ready within a week, and the drawings matted after two

weeks. She would coordinate with the design team members, who would help to install the work the day before the show was to open. Ward said his publicity team would start working on fliers and invitations, as well as the wall text. Timeka wanted to consult with the other members of her host team to think of "something neat" for the reception. Kelly, who had been taking notes, produced the brief shown in Figure 2.3.

AN EXHIBITION TIMETABLE AND CHECKLIST

Exhibition time frames vary according to their complexity. Small shows can be moved along with relative speed; an extravaganza may take months to put together. A timetable and checklist that gives dates when each task begins and when it should be completed complements the brief. Curators can consult with each team to determine how long various tasks will take and who will be responsible for them.

In planning a timetable, work backward. Decide when the exhibition will open, and then plan what must be completed the day of the opening, the week before, two weeks before, and so on. Checklists break large duties down into specific tasks and due dates that provide a sense of accomplishment as they are completed (see Figure 2.4). Without a clear timetable and a checklist, momentum can waver and commitment may languish. As students and teams complete their tasks, they should formally "sign off" on the timetable, thereby acknowledging their successful achievement and receiving praise from their team and their teacher. Some tasks may also require short reports on what was learned, decided, or attained. Teachers can help to maintain a realistic time frame and spur students to move forward by encouraging them to meet deadlines.

Tracks for different tasks or teams can help to clarify duties. Tracks can be kept on separate timetables or color-coded on a master timetable. Larger tasks should have checkpoints for students to report when they are a third of the way or half done.

Unforeseen delays can disrupt the timetable. Build in extra time to buffer them. Tasks often take more time than students predict. They may need reminders to stay on schedule. When schedules appear to lag or are not met, curators may need to commit additional resources and people to help. Occasionally, a student will lose interest or "shut down" to attract attention. Acknowledging how important that person is, and how integral to the success of the exhibition his or her contribution is, often is enough get the student back on track. Pointing out that another student can take over his or her duties, if necessary, raises the ante a notch. Actually reassigning the duties

Figure 2.3. Outline of a Sample Exhibition Brief

BEFORE MEETING WITH OTHER TEAMS

Curators:

- Discuss various possible themes and select one.
- Determine type of exhibition and venue.
- Establish criteria that reflect the theme, type, and venue.
- Select artwork that best fulfills the criteria of the theme. (Eighteen out of 29 works were selected.)

END OF 1ST WEEK:

Curators: Explain "Hidden Images" theme; accession the artwork.
Design: Show exhibition design to curators.
Installation: Work on labels; begin matting.
Publicity: Work on flyers; discuss text.
Reception: Plan special event for reception.

END OF 2ND WEEK

Curators: Check with teams to see who is on task.
Design: Make any adjustments in design; prepare venue.
Installation: Continue matting; print text.
Publicity: Give text to installers to print and mount.
Reception: Rehearse docents for reception; plan music and refreshments.

END OF 3RD WEEK

Curators: Check with teams to see who is on task.
Design: Help installation team install artwork.
Installation: Install artwork; make final adjustments.
Publicity: Distribute invitations; publicize show during morning announcements.
Reception: Prepare music and refreshments; continue to rehearse docents.

RECEPTION:

Curators: Check with teams to see who is on task; fill in as needed.
Design: Mingle with guests.
Installation: Photograph installation and reception.
Publicity: Make informal assessments of guests' reactions.
Reception: Prompt guests with questions that make them view the artwork more deeply; serve refreshments; play evocative music.

DISMANTLE SHOW:

Curators: Return artwork to Mrs. Bailey.
Design: Clear and clean space at end of show.
Installation: Take down artwork at end of show.
Publicity: Take down signage, text, and fliers.
Reception: Clean up refreshments after reception.

Figure 2.4. A Sample Checklist for Student Exhibitions

Activity	Who does it?	Done
Decide focus, theme, or content of show	————	————
Determine format to be used	————	————
Select title	————	————
Order or make title letters	————	————
Prepare press release and exhibit announcement	————	————
Start plans for reception if planned	————	————
Select jurors if used	————	————
Decide on number of works of art	————	————
Select work or jury work	————	————
Have release forms signed	————	————
Put together labels and other text	————	————
Type labels on computer, mount labels on card	————	————
Decide presentation of each piece (size, frame, etc.)	————	————
Lay out exhibit	————	————
Mount work ready for framing	————	————
Clean frames	————	————
Install exhibit	————	————
Install labels	————	————
Adjust lighting	————	————
Last-minute cleanup	————	————
Make corrections as necessary	————	————
Photograph students with artwork for press release	————	————
Document show	————	————
Remind teachers/students of end of exhibit	————	————
Dismantle show	————	————
Wrap items, return to students or teacher	————	————
Make repairs to exhibit space	————	————

Source: Taylor, 1992

to another student may be the last step. If there are major delays and the timetable cannot be met, the exhibition's opening date can be pushed back. This should only be done as a last resort, as it will disrupt future exhibitions.

USING A SCALE MODEL OF THE EXHIBITION SPACE

Once an installation design has been decided upon for the exhibition, a scale model of the exhibition area, particularly if it has an unusual floor plan, provides several benefits to designers. It permits them to quickly rearrange miniature-scale artworks into a variety of configurations, provides a literal overview of the entire exhibition that adds an architectural dimension to the exhibition process, and enables designers to check technical features, such as lighting. The floor space of the actual exhibition area can be kept free until installation details have been finalized. Graph paper helps to set the scale and demarcate the eye-level horizontal line on where most works will be centered. Models may be simple paper assemblies or more elaborate foamcore constructions.

Models of exhibitions allow students to quickly "sketch" several installation alternatives; discover and solve problems; and present visual examples that other students and their teachers can readily understand, discuss, and decide upon. Several students can work on a single model, or each individual can produce his or her own example. Models illustrate that there are innumerable ways that art can be arranged, and that each way communicates its own distinct message. Different ideas can also be easily synthesized from several models.

Using a scale model helped the design team in Mrs. Bailey's class consider alternative installation designs, as we see as the scenario continues:

> Gabrielle, Nadi, Jamal, and Rachel, the design team for "Hidden Meanings," have already decided on a comparative installation design in which contrasting works will be paired to emphasize their symbolic content.
>
> Mrs. Bailey provided the team with a scale model of the gallery made from foamcore. The sides could be unpinned to fold down flat. Although design teams often make tiny scale drawings of each work of art to arrange in a model, Nadi photographed the drawings with a digital camera and made tiny, scaled-down images of them using one of the room's computers. Gabrielle and Rachel glued the appropriate pairs to paper rectangles to represent the mattes.
>
> The team started sorting the drawings into pairs. "These two go together," Rachel observed, "because they both have plants and flowers."

"Here's another pair with graffiti symbols," Nadi chimed in.

"I've got a couple with animals," Gabrielle offered.

When they had paired all the drawings, they huddled around the flattened-out scale model, discussing what they thought each pair of drawings meant and how they related to other pairs. They positioned the miniature drawings against the walls of the miniature gallery and immediately realized that they would have to use freestanding panels if they wanted to have enough space to hang nine pairs of drawings. Jamal folded three pieces of paper to represent the panels and placed them near the windows in the scale model.

They arranged the pairs of scaled-down drawings in the model. Jamal said, "You know, it's obvious some of these drawings are about personal stuff, like Sharon's; she has her stuffed toys and ballet slippers. And others, like Aaron's, have more serious symbols."

"I see what you mean," Nadi said. "Putting two drawings with animals in them together 'telegraphs' stuff about animals. No one will look for any deeper meaning."

Gabrielle mused out loud, "Suppose we put them in pairs that really didn't go together, like Aaron's and Sharon's. Aaron's drawing has a lot of deep, dark imagery, while Sharon's is obviously a lot lighter."

"I like that," Nadi replied. "By putting them together, we can contrast them more. It will make people think, 'What's going on here?'"

"Aaron's and Sharon's drawings contrast a lot—angry and happy," Rachel added. "But we can mix it up. I mean, make each pair contrast in different ways so people have to figure out each one."

The four designers immediately set about arranging different pairs to produce visual contrasts and symbolic tensions. They had a lot of fun thinking up unusual juxtapositions. Then they went back to the model gallery and began rearranging the miniature pairs again. After going through several permutations, and even considering which work should be on the left and which on the right, they placed their selections in the final positions.

They took their final design back to the curatorial team, and Gabrielle explained their comparative design strategy and how different pairs represented different metaphorical relationships. The student curators liked the idea very much and gave their approval.

CONCLUSION

Exhibition designs organize art conceptually and visually. The history of art exhibition evolved from an ostentatious and cluttered salon display to a more austere, linear formalism in which works are visually isolated from one another in order to be viewed separately. As contemporary art itself becomes more "viewer friendly" by actively engaging the viewer, contemporary exhibitions strive toward more compelling, thought-provoking relationships. In Cases 2, Part II, I present six familiar types of exhibition design: salon, linear, sequential, comparative, synoptic, and contextual. By working with various types of installations, students can discover how different physical arrangements affect a variety of conceptual and aesthetic experiences.

Even the simplest exhibitions need to be thoughtfully designed to exemplify their themes and to present artwork to its best advantage. Good designs demand good plans. An exhibition requires an exhibition brief and a timetable to be successful. A brief lays out an orderly sequence of tasks, duties, and roles. A timetable creates a reasonable schedule for completing each task.

CHAPTER 3

Exhibition Installation

The third phase in exhibiting art involves the actual installation of the works in a chosen space. Venues vary widely, from simple bulletin boards to full-scale galleries and sites in the community. Wherever the venue, a successful installation requires being well organized, as Diaz (1998) explains:

> It is crucial to have one adult, the installation captain, directing the efforts of the rest of the installation crew, which will be a combination of students, teachers and parents. Include people in this part of the project who like to work with their hands, and have skills in design, layout, installation and building. The ability to solve problems and be flexible when things don't go together exactly as planned is equally important. (p. 44)

Installing an exhibition entails several steps:

1. Accessioning each work of art
2. Preparing the art for exhibition
3. Preparing the space for exhibition
4. Creating signage and other text
5. Arranging and installing the art

ACCESSIONING ART FOR EXHIBITION

Documenting the history of each work of art is important to art history as a whole. Museums and galleries register works of art when they acquire them by recording the pertinent information related to the works, including their provenance, or history, in their accession records. The provenance tells who previously owned the work, what collections and exhibitions have included it, what artists might have been influenced by it, and other interesting facts related to its history.

Accessioning art is good practice whether or not the work is exhibited. Accession records should include the names of the artist and of the artwork; its medium, size, and description; and the dates when it was created and acquired. Accession records of student art may also include the lesson concept, any student comments, and perhaps even a small sketch of the work (see Figure 3.1 for a sample accession form). Accessioning each work as students complete it provides them with a brief but reflective summary and collects their thoughts for the closure discussion.

Accessioning lends the work of art an aura of authenticity that students appreciate, especially if the teacher makes a point of saving the completed accession forms. The accession form becomes the work of art's "birth certificate." Whether to accession certain works such as sketches can lead to interesting aesthetic discussions. What makes something a work of art?

Each work of art in an exhibition should be accessioned, if only to make certain it will be returned to its rightful owner. One copy of the accession

Figure 3.1. An Accession Certificate

ACCESSION CERTIFICATE   Date _____

Name of Artist _____

Title of Artwork_____

Description of Artwork _____

_____

_____

Dimensions (in inches and centimeters) _____

Art Medium _____

Artistic Concept _____

_____

Artist's Comments _____

_____

_____

                                              sketch of artwork

Teacher's Name _____ Room # _____

form stays with the work of art (usually attached to its reverse side), while the curators catalog a second copy with their brief. The artist might receive a third copy to keep as a receipt. Curators and the development team should both keep master lists of all the works.

PREPARING ART FOR EXHIBITION

Preparing the art for exhibition comes next. In schools, art selected for display often arrives "as is"—unmatted, unframed, and not ready for display. If the artwork is not ready for hanging, the curators, the design team, the installation team, or a combination of them must prepare it for being shown.

The first requirement of exhibiting is to attract the viewers' attention. Even a modest effort at good presentation pays off handsomely. Mounts, borders, and mattes can be attractive without being elaborate or expensive. Young children can learn to mount their own flat artwork on larger sheets of paper. They enjoy picking their own colors for their mounts and borders and decorating them with scraps of construction paper or with rubber stamps. Sharon Clohessy (personal correspondence, 2003) suggests writing poems, messages, or the concept statement of the lesson around the border. Repeating patterns can also be added to borders. The borders can become progressively more complex as time goes on.

Young children may have difficulty aligning their art evenly on a larger mount. Their first efforts can be "crazy mounts" that are glued down intentionally askew. When all their work is crazy mounted in bright colors and randomly hung on a colorful background, the whole display seems to dance.

As students become more skillful, they can improvise borders by gluing strips of paper or poster board around the artworks' edges. Square overlaps eventually give way to mitered corners as their skills improve. Borders also provide a flexible and inexpensive way to learn to double-mount artwork without extensive measuring and cutting. Children especially enjoy trimming the precut strips with deckle scissors to give them a decorative touch.

Students also enjoy constructing more elaborate presentations using a variety of materials. Wallpaper, wrapping paper, paste-grained designs, and collages offer imaginative alternatives. Printing companies often have remnants of specialty papers that make ideal borders. Precut poster-board window mattes are inexpensive yet lend immediate prestige to two-dimensional work. Many cultures display their art in their own distinctive ways. Japanese sumi-e ink paintings and Persian miniatures, for example, are mounted on scrolls of gilded paper or brocaded fabric. These expensive materials can be improvised from decorative wrapping paper and wallpaper.

With proper training, middle school students can learn to use a matte cutter. Cutting window mattes is a practice best reserved for mature students who can be closely supervised and are able to master the technical refinements of measuring and cutting.

Although most schools cannot afford to glaze and frame student artwork, some art teachers maintain a stock of inexpensive frames for student use while their art is being displayed. These frames can be used over and over again while students learn about the skills and aesthetics related to well-presented art. Student art clubs, art booster clubs, or parent-teacher organizations may be willing to contribute funds for mattes and frames, particularly when exhibitions advocate for the art program, build student esteem, and make the school more attractive. Framing shops occasionally have sales or may even contribute frames to an art program. Graphik Dimensions Limited (www.pictureframes.com) offers a varied stock of component frames that can be assembled easily and later disassembled for the next show. They are reusable, durable, and relatively inexpensive and come in many colors, finishes, and styles.

Michael Gettings, who teaches art in Chesterfield County, Virginia, described how his students prepare their art for exhibition:

> I had an art club that met once a week for 30 minutes. I showed them how to mount flat work on construction paper (no matte cutting), and how and where to place name tags. I chose a couple of students to type information into a student database that created the name tags. The database helped to keep track of the students—heaven forbid if I missed a student in the show! These mounting sessions went extremely well. In a 30-minute period, the club could mount and tag more work than I could do in a month. I tried to get the students to do as much as possible. I felt that it gave them a better sense of what an art show is all about and a greater sense of ownership for the show. I know many teachers use parent volunteers, but for the big show, I relied on the students. (personal correspondence, 2000)

PREPARING THE SITE FOR EXHIBITION

The third step focuses on preparing the space for exhibition. At its simplest, this entails clearing and cleaning the site. While the cleanup team from the previous show should "leave the area as they found it," the site usually needs at least a thorough inspection. Any detritus from the previous show should be removed at this point.

Adding natural and manufactured objects to the site offers accents that echo the art. Real plants harmonize beautifully with paintings of flowers. Visitors enjoy seeing the objects or even the actual setup that inspired still-life drawings. Historical and cultural objects and documents can complement art by reflecting a certain time or place. An installation can carry through a motif suggested by the theme. Art inspired by music might be arranged on music stands. Drawings of Greek amphorae could have a Greek key motif running behind them. A blue background will suggest a watery environment for *gyotaku* fish prints.

Some themes or installation designs may inspire extensive site preparation, including painting walls and adjusting lighting, which usually requires teacher approval, administrative permission, and custodial assistance. When students gain a reputation for outstanding exhibitions and responsible and effective presentations, they are likely to gain the confidence and support of the school administration. Many exhibition sites, such as the school's main office, cannot be altered. The art usually must be hung from the picture hangers already in place.

Display Panels

Display panels add to the amount of space available within an exhibition area. They also make the physical layout of installations more flexible. They are generally used in open-traffic areas, not in hallways, where they would present a safety hazard or where the art might be damaged. Larger shows usually demand additional display panels. Display panels should be durable because they are frequently moved and must last for many years. They should be lightweight, double sided, and made of a material to which artwork may be easily and securely attached. Heavyweight and dense surfaces such as plywood, Masonite, and chipboard are unsuitable, unless they are covered with a tightly woven fabric to which artwork can be hung. Hollow doors can be used for display panels, however, pins and nails will damage them. Artwork must be attached with masking tape or other adhesives. Heavy pieces can be hung from strings or wires attached to the unseen, top edge of the door. Pulp particle (homosote) boards come in 4' × 8' sheets, but their soft edges can be easily damaged. Frames made from routed 1' × 2' strips provide the desired durability. The full-size panels are quite heavy, but they may be cut down to convenient dimensions (perhaps 2' × 6') that are lighter in weight. Pegboard and wire lath, also set in frames, offer two other durable alternatives. A wide variety of commercial hanging systems exist, and others can be improvised at modest cost.

Art hung on walls or on other large, flat areas can be viewed as a whole and then examined more closely. Teachers often employ panels to increase their exhibition area. Two panels, such as hollow doors, can be made freestanding by joining their common edges at right angles to each other (\/) with hinges and pins, while three panels can form a very stable screenlike configuration (/\/) or a triangular column. Four panels may be anchored along a single edge to form an intersection (+) or along four edges to form a cubic column. These structures can in turn guide viewers past works of art in a prescribed fashion while forming self-contained, synoptic vignettes or creating corners that hide works until they are ready to be revealed. Screen panels should be staggered when they run parallel to each other. In this way, they form little alcoves where a few works can share their influence.

When intersecting panels (+) are placed next to each other, they act as a flat wall punctuated by perpendicular panels (+ + +). Viewers may pause as they walk by, but their progress is generally aligned with the "wall." When the units are turned, they create little pockets (× × × ×) that encourage viewers to discover a more circuitous route by weaving through them. Triangular prisms also create different effects when their edges or faces point toward one another. Another interesting configuration joins two angled pairs with a flat panel (> – <) that provides maximum viewing areas on two sides and smaller viewing niches on the ends, while creating a stable, free-standing unit.

Art That Stands Out

Sculpture and other three-dimensional art require special consideration in order to be viewed properly, yet kept from becoming obstacles to pedestrian traffic. Installation designers should think about these questions:

- Will viewers be permitted to walk around the work of art, viewing it from all sides, or will it be located near a wall or in a corner, allowing only a partial view?
- How will it be lighted?
- How will viewers be guided from art on the walls to a freestanding work in the middle of the room?
- Will several three-dimensional works be grouped together?

Art that poses safety problems because of sharp edges, moving or electrical parts, or other dangerous features should be isolated in corners or on stands where viewers cannot touch it. Small items are often more interesting if they are clustered together in showcases.

Electronic Media and Performance Art

Four-dimensional art adds time to the artistic and aesthetic equations by introducing motion through space. Videotaped vignettes and computer-generated art intentionally push the boundaries of traditional art. Although these media are quite contemporary, many students are as technically and financially able to explore them as they are any other artistic medium. Video monitors and VCRs can be installed easily in a school gallery. Some schools broadcast video and electronic art to all their classroom monitors through their local area network (LAN).

Performance art has become a standard art form in the past three decades. Whether it is scripted or improvised, careful planning for the space where it will be performed is needed. Interaction with viewers and their responses often constitute an important aspect of performance art. Safety is always a prime consideration, particularly if surprises or unanticipated reactions make up part of the performance.

Lighting

Lighting dramatically affects the impact of art. As Janet Turner (1998) points out:

> The lighting director is, like the exhibition designer, an intermediary between the visitor and the work, both bringing the visitor closer to the work on show, and enabling the work to communicate most appropriately with the visitor. Putting this into practice is one of the most exciting aspects of lighting design. (p. 15)

Natural lighting from skylights and windows provides the truest interpretation of colors and three-dimensional forms. However, hallways, and even classrooms and open areas, are often underlit and gloomy and may not show art to its best advantage. Nevertheless, lighting need not be left to chance. Florescent lighting casts a bluish glow that emphasizes blues and purples, at the cool end of the spectrum. Incandescent lights, which throw off a warm radiance, can be used to balance cool florescent lights. Full-spectrum florescent lights are more expensive, but they are well worth the additional expense and should be used in galleries and settings where art frequently appears. If track lighting is available, spotlights, floodlights, and pastel lights provide options to dramatize, create moods, and attract attention. Often lighting cannot be adjusted until the artwork is in place, but it can be planned well beforehand. Students can experiment with penlights on the scale model of the show. While lighting adjustments should be left to the custodians for safety reasons, students can still actively plan and direct its use as part of their installation design.

SELECTING A TITLE FOR THE EXHIBITION

Selecting a title can lead to endless debate. Assigning the task to a specific group of two or three students expedites the process greatly. They should have the job of creating the signage as well. Making signage often cuts down on verbiage.

A snappy title attracts attention, piques curiosity, and gives the viewer an immediate hint of the intent and content of the show. It can be a catchy phrase, a pun or other form of wordplay, an abbreviated description, or even a provocative question. The theme type of the show or its style of installation may suggest the form or flavor of the title. An issue-oriented show might shout a protest, as in *Pollution Kills!* while an installation juxtaposing words and pictures may play upon its comparative character with *Versus Verses*.

A title sharpens the theme to a precise point, but it should not be mistaken for the theme. Students frequently say, "We've got a great title for the show!" The teacher's response is, "Wonderful! But what is the theme?" The theme involves much more than is usually expressed in a title.

CREATING SIGNAGE AND TEXT

Simple signage adds to the exhibition's immediate impact. A short title written in large letters and describing the theme announces the exhibition simply and can be read from a distance. One or more simple statements printed in a large-point type can elaborate on the theme and may be the only labeling needed. A thematic icon repeated in publicity, signage, and invitations gives a recognizable motif that ties various aspects of the exhibition together.

Signage and text support the intent of the theme and extent of the installation. *Signage* refers to simple phrases, such as a title, presented in large-scale typefaces that can be seen from a distance. *Text* is writing, usually in paragraph form, that explains main aspects of the exhibition, such as the theme or specific sections of it. It may be presented in somewhat oversized (16- to 24-point) typefaces. Hope Irvine (1999) suggests providing "wall text that underlines the goals of each lesson through which the works were produced. Viewers have criteria by which to judge the quality of instruction rather than just enjoying works by students they assume are 'talented'" (p. 1).

Signage and text represent another dimension of the exhibition that facilitates continuity between works of art, much as punctuation does between words in a well-structured paragraph. In many respects, the installation design guides what will be written in the text and signage by introducing, explaining, describing, and questioning individual works and groups of works. Curators should keep this in mind and work closely with their design and publicity teams as they write supporting text.

Labels are captions placed near specific works of art. They are usually printed in 12- to 16-point type, which is easily readable but does not distract from the work of art itself. Labeling represents an art form in itself. Labels may be simple, including only the artist's name and the work's title. They are sometimes referred to as "tombstones," for obvious reasons. Labels may also go into greater detail, with the artist's comments, additional information, or explanatory notes. They should be to the point and written with the viewers' reading ability in mind. Generally, students can write their own labels, but other students (or, possibly, the teacher) should check them for spelling, grammar, and readability. With dozens of fonts to choose from, computers make attractive labels easy to produce, easy to read, and consistent with the art and the theme of the exhibition. Bilingual or multilingual labels offer other possibilities, especially if the artwork is inspired by another culture or the venue has a large multicultural population.

Prompts help the students to focus on the content of their labels. Salient questions or phrases that require completion ("If my painting could talk, it would say . . .") create a common format and encourage deeper thought. When students help develop these questions and phrases, they should ask themselves how the questions and phrases can help promote the theme for their viewers. Labels also can be written as questions that grab the viewers' attention and create more interaction.

Serrell's *Exhibit Labels: An Interpretive Approach* (1996) provides an excellent guide to understanding the purpose of labels and how to write them. She cites several types of labels, including title labels (or signage), which iden-tify the name of the exhibition; introductory or orientation labels, which set up the organization and tone of the exhibition; section or group labels, which inform viewers about specific subgroupings of works; and captions, which are labels for specific works of art.

Labels are optional. Some exhibitions prove to be stronger when their written comments are limited to signage. When exhibitions occupy heavy-traffic areas, such as hallways, labels should be used sparingly. In these busy locations, students will not and cannot stop to read them.

ARRANGING AND INSTALLING THE ART

Like all the other phases of mounting an exhibition, the actual installation is a team effort. In some instances, particularly when the show is small, the design team transforms itself into the installation team, because it saves time and those students have the clearest idea of how they want the show to look.

However, when the exhibition is large scale, particularly if there are many works of art to mount or matte, additional students may make up a separate installation team. They can usually begin their work of cataloging and preparing the art for hanging as soon as the curatorial team announces the exhibition's theme. The installation team must, of course, coordinate with the design team regarding any special display features, but it can often have the art ready for hanging by the time the design team finalizes its plans. The in-stallation team should also coordinate with the publicity team to prepare the actual signage and text used in the show.

In practice, many hands make light work, and the design team will very likely join the installation team for the actual installation. Both teams need to cooperate with each other. The design team must make a special effort to be receptive to any suggestions and flexible in their attitudes. If the design team rotates to become the installation team for the next exhibition, its members may gain a greater appreciation of what the installation team does.

To those in charge of installing an exhibition, Diaz (1998) offers advice:

> Have the floor plans and inventory list in hand and make copies for everyone involved in installation. Give clear directions before beginning to install the exhibit so that everyone knows the process to be followed and who is responsible for each part of the installation. Encourage people to work in teams so they can help one another if they have difficulties. The installation team captain will periodically check in with everyone on the crew to ensure that they have the needed tools and are comfortable with the tasks. (p. 44)

The students at the Ross School in East Hampton, New York, produce elaborate exhibitions of professional artists in their school gallery. Laurel G., a student, describes their process for selecting and installing artwork in Case 3.1 in Part II.

Hanging Flat Artwork

In many instances, flat artwork can be attached to masonry walls and wooden surfaces with masking tape rolled into cylinders (curls). Double-sided foam tape also works well but is more expensive. There are many other kinds of adhesives with which to experiment. Administrators sometimes object to tape and adhesives, which can damage painted surfaces. This is actually an excellent argument for installing cork strips or extruded-metal hanging strips in halls throughout the school. Cork strips are usually placed above eye level so when the top edges of artwork are pinned to it, the artwork settles to the correct visual level.

Extruded-metal strips are installed near the ceiling. Artwork can then be hung at any height from strings and brackets that hook over the metal strip. With a little practice, students can learn to attach brackets in the metal strips using poles. For obvious safety reasons, they should not climb on ladders or stools to set the brackets.

Thin cotton string, kite string, and wire offer good hanging properties. Monofilament fishing line and nylon string are difficult to tie and keep tied, and thin monofilament will stretch under heavy loads. Strings taped directly to the back of artwork tend to slip or pull free. A paper clip bent into the shape of an inverted number 2 and taped to the back of the artwork will secure the work better, make adjusting the hanging string easier, and allow for quick dismantling.

Artwork is frequently attached to bulletin boards and cork strips with pins and staples. Push pins and beaded (map) pins have tapered points that can loosen and fall out after a few days. T-pins or L-pins work better. If they are too long, they can be shortened with wire snips. Very small, headed wire brads hold artwork more securely, especially if it is matted or heavy, because they are not tapered. Tiny ½" × #19 brads are about the same gauge as a pushpin and will not damage a cork surface. The brads can be removed easily with pliers. Students from the installation team should be assigned to inspect and rehang each morning any artwork that has fallen or shifted overnight.

Staples anchor lightweight art mounted on paper sufficiently but do not drive deeply enough to hold matted or heavy work. Heavy-duty staples can handle thicker, heavier work, but they are not very attractive. Some teachers position the staples perpendicular to the edge of the work so only one tooth goes into the cork surface to its full depth while the other tooth grips the artwork securely. Colored staples offer a decorative touch. Care should always be taken to ensure that the art is level and spaced properly.

Many teachers use mural paper on bulletin boards to enliven the artwork or set a mood. Laying mural paper directly on the floor in front of the bulletin board or wall where the art will be displayed allows students, particularly younger students, to easily envision how it will look and to rearrange and align their work freely without climbing on chairs to put it up. Once they have decided on its placement, they can attach the artwork with tape curls or glue. Then, with adult help, the whole mural can be lifted into place and stapled securely. Folding over the top edge of the mural paper once or twice reinforces it. A wood lattice strip inside the fold makes it easy for two adults to pick up. The lattice strip slides out once the mural paper is secured in place.

If students cannot reach high enough to hang their art, teachers, custodians, or parent volunteers can help out. The students nevertheless should be in charge of directing the installation.

In Mrs. Bailey's class the installation team worked with the design team to install the "Hidden Meanings" exhibition:

> Molly, a curator, joined Kendra, Geoff, and Juan to form the installation team. They spent two afternoons matting the 18 symbolic drawings that would eventually be exhibited. Kendra typed and printed the identification labels and glued them onto cardboard mounts. The design team told Geoff and Juan that they would need three display panels, which they moved from Mrs. Bailey's art supply room to the school lobby.
>
> When the design team decided on their installation design, they showed the foamcore mock-up to Molly, Kendra, Geoff, and Juan; explained their idea; and asked for their opinions. The installers agreed with the basic design.

The installation team used a grid system to arrange the show. They knew the number of works of art and their relative positions. Molly and Juan measured off on grid paper where each would be placed and figured out the actual measurements for the walls. All four students hung plumb lines representing the midlines between each pair of drawings. Mrs. Bailey said the drawings should be hung at eye level. Kendra calculated a typical student's eye level at 5' 4" and decided that the top edge of the mats therefore should be 5' 10" above the floor. Geoff and Juan agreed. They stretched horizontal strings along the four walls at the specified height. Mrs. Bailey showed them how to put weights on the ends of the strings so they would remain taut and straight.

The four students took turns pinning the drawings and text in place with pushpins. Two students held the work while another pinned. The third student acted as a "spotter" from across the room, suggesting slight corrections in level and spacing. When they were finished they removed the strings, and the design team looked the installation over.

Juan pointed out that people coming in the main entrance would first encounter a pair of drawings that were pleasant enough but not very provocative. He suggested that a dramatic pair be substituted. The design team tried out the change and agreed that it made a bigger impression.

In Case 3.2 in Part II, Michael Gettings provides another example of students' installing their artwork.

Installing 3-D and 4-D Art

Some three-dimensional art, such as masks or reliefs, can be mounted on walls just like two-dimensional art. However, many three-dimensional works pose unique problems because they are freestanding. They must be placed high enough to be seen easily yet secured well enough not to be toppled. Tables are usually too low (except for young children) to provide an effective installation. Platforms, such as boxes of different heights, placed on tables can raise artwork to appropriate heights for viewing. Permanent showcases provide another alternative, but these require a steady supply of three-dimensional exhibits. When only a few three-dimensional works are exhibited, plinths, pedestals, and columns provide attractive supports. The artworks should be secured to their bases with museum wax, tape, or hot glue, and the pedestal itself should be firmly anchored with an internal sandbag or a base that is wider that the diameter of the column. Mobiles should be hung well above head level or in areas where traffic is not permitted.

As alluded to earlier, electronic media allows artists and exhibitors to add a fourth dimension—time (and thereby, movement)—to art. Audio- and video-tapes, QuickTime video and programmed PowerPoint, and other computer-based presentations have opened the door to all kinds of new exhibition modes. The Internet has also expanded exhibition possibilities exponentially. Moreover, when access is provided, viewers can interact with work of art more directly. Many types of four-dimensional presentations can be looped to play continuously and, therefore, require little maintenance. However, expensive equipment does need to be protected.

Performance art merges art and drama. While performance art can occur at any time or anywhere in order to appear spontaneous and to surprise, if not startle, its audience, the exhibition reception often provides an ideal occasion to complement the static art that is also in the exhibition.

INTERACTIVE INSTALLATION:
THE VIEWER PLAYS AN ACTIVE ROLE

What better way could there be to exhibit masks or costumes than with cele-brations, parades, and dances? Many kinds of art naturally elevate the spirit. Incorporating them into festive rituals and ceremonies makes perfect sense. Newly made musical instruments demand musical performances! Whirligigs need to be spun. Toys and games must be played with by children. Animated art requires that artists and viewers alike interact with it.

Some installations invite viewers to explore, discover, invent, mimic, role-play, or be artistically creative. Optical illusions require viewer interaction to work but need not actually be touched. Viewers can use tools, such as special eyeglasses, mirrors, and lenses, to view art in special ways. Props complement and dramatize the artwork as well.

Regarding interactive exhibitions, Czajkowski and Sikora (2003) note that labels are not a good match for every aesthetic outcome. Viewers need some control over their own experience and the variety of their experiences. As the authors point out, "Something to touch in an art museum is a really interesting thing" (n.p.). In an exhibition of Edgar Degas's dancers, tall mir-rors, a ballet barre, and footprints of ballet positions on the floor drew viewers into the kinesthetic as well as visual experience.

Even for traditional art, contemporary exhibition installations frequently encourage interaction between viewers and the art. Electronic devices invite viewers to cast opinions, answer questions, and ask for more information. PowerPoint presentations on laptops help make interaction easy. Hypermedia allows students to pursue ideas and questions to a considerable depth.

The interaction need not be direct. Viewers can answer questions or make sketches from a sheet or booklet they receive when they enter the exhibition.

Puzzles or riddles may ask viewers to look more closely at the works of art to discover latent meanings. Informative labeling placed near works provides background, suggestive prompts, and other content.

Diaz (1998) notes:

> Interactive exhibits invite visitors to learn by doing, not just seeing and hearing. They attempt to encourage visitors to use a variety of skills, aside from just looking, observing, reading and reflecting. They require visitors to use their bodies in some way to gain information. Hands-on exhibits incorporate sound, movement, color, smell, texture, light, and a variety of forms, with 2 and 3 dimensional design. Very often, successful interactive exhibits ask visitors to become part of the environment, and they make learning into a game or a discovery. [Interactive exhibits strive] to convey a message, stimulate the senses, challenge the imagination, excite new perceptions, [and] effectively relate information. (p. 32)

Case 3.3 in Part II describes how artist Martina Lopez created an interactive installation with advice from a group of children at the Art Institute of Chicago.

EVENT OR PERFORMANCE: CREATE A FANTASY

Lord Byron once observed, "Art is the life we imagine." Art is creative, and art exhibitions should be as well. Children love to give free rein to their imagination. Exhibition gives them comparable arenas in the real world.

Gibson (1961) speaks of "making the familiar strange, and making the strange familiar" (p. 35). Some art exhibitions try to conjure up unorthodox points of view. They provoke questions rather than resolving them. Paradox always intrigues us, whether it is the ambiguity of a Necker cube visual illusion, the surreal enigma of a painting by René Magritte, or the double coding of a Barbara Kruger poster. Paradox provides rich themes to explore in art exhibitions as well. They require students to understand them well enough to present them to others effectively but without giving away the trick.

Everyone loves a good joke. The inherent contradiction, the surprise ending, and the humorous absurdity make jokes a gold mine of exhibition themes. Puns, riddles, even limericks, can be points of departure for works of art, as well as for clever exhibitions.

Traditionally, artists have served as society's bellwethers, showing us the possibilities of the future in their art. Timely exhibitions have always been crucial to the avant-garde, for their prescient insights cannot wait. Children are deeply concerned about the future because, as the wit says, that is where they are going to spend the rest of their lives. The future abounds with themes for exhibitions, be they speculations, prophesies, hopes, desires, or dreams.

All the arts find expression in performance, ritual, and celebration, yet they break away from the traditional exhibition format of pictures on the walls. Nori Thorne, a middle school art teacher in Beallsville, Maryland, explains,

> Most of my exhibits have a performance component. *Friday After-noon at JPMS Pond*, a pointillist installation with life-sized Seurat figures [featured live] picnickers dressed in 19th-century costumes. It was one of those happy, infrequent events in which everything went smoothly. There was even some magic: when the chorus sang about wild geese, a perfect V of them flew overhead, and when one of my students, dressed in a bustle and straw hat threw her fishing line into the pond to catch a pretend fish, she caught a real one! (Personal correspondence, October 2003).

Students immediately respond to using art actively and interactively with excitement, imagination, and enthusiasm

AMBIENCE

Creating an overall atmosphere that evokes a certain emotional response can bring the experience of art to its fullest realization. Lighting, props, wall colors and textures, text, and the installation itself all contribute to infusing a subliminal current that instills a mood in the exhibition space (see Figure 3.2 and Case 3.4 in Part II). The behavior of the docents and curators can further add to the tone of the event.

Ambience should be subtle. It should not detract from the art or the experience. It should nudge the viewers, not hit them over the head. A slight change in wall color or the use of spotlights instead of floodlights can make all the difference.

The intended mood of the exhibition needs to be well considered while it is being designed and installed:

- In what order will viewers encounter various works of art?
- How will their feelings change from one work to the next?
- How will these little experiences combine to make an overall experience?
- What will be the nature of that whole experience?

CONCLUSION

Students, not their teacher, should design their own exhibitions. Teachers may instruct, supervise, and make suggestions, but as much as possible, they

Figure 3.2. The House of Mysteries, Pompeii, installation in the café. The Ross School, East Hampton, New York. Jennifer Cross and her students transformed their café into a Roman villa.

Photo: The Ross School

should allow students to make the decisions about how the art should be arranged and installed and who should perform which duties. Finally, students should undertake the actual installation themselves. They need a variety of skills to install art in an effective manner. By starting with modestly scaled installations requiring only simple skills, and progressively building up their abilities, students can successfully install every show. The theme should be posted prominently where everyone can refer to it.

Even young children can install their art as a group, making decisions about where various works of art should be placed. Rose Martin, an elementary art teacher in Fenton, Michigan, has her students keep a portfolio. "They look over their year's work and select a piece. If they can't decide, I might suggest a couple of pieces, but they make the final choice" (personal correspondence, October 2002). As they become familiar with the exhibition process, and if each child has had several opportunities to exhibit during the school year, decisions may be made by the whole group, but the actual installation can be turned over to a few designated individuals. Eventually, everyone will acquire the skills, motivation, and maturity to undertake installation on his or her own in small groups, with less direct supervision by the teacher. The teacher, of course, must approve the students' plans and preparations before they begin these more independent installations.

Certain kinds of exhibitions, such as *Student Artist of the Week* or *Famous Artist of the Week*, allow students to acquire installation skills working in groups of two or three in a specified venue, usually within the classroom. Ongoing formats can be easily assessed and indicate when students are ready to tackle bigger tasks.

Installations can be creative and imaginative. Interactive and performance installations make viewers a part of the art and transform art into an experience. Curators and designers should consider the ambience of the setting to create a mood conducive to the theme of the exhibition.

CHAPTER 4

Exhibition Publicity

Viewers are as necessary to an exhibition as the art itself. They are its essential reason for being. Curators must consider who will view the art when deciding on a theme, selecting specific works, and designing the installation. Everything is a channel to attracting viewers, informing them in interesting ways, and influencing them toward positive ends. Therefore, it is important to know who the viewers will be and to anticipate how and why they will view the art. In schools, students may be the most immediate audience, but teachers, parents, and administrators will also see the show. In wider venues or in school activities attended by the public, even more varied audiences will make up the viewing public.

A SHIFT IN PERSPECTIVE:
TAKING THE VIEWER'S POINT OF VIEW

Up to this point, curators and designers have been asserting their own expressions and their own points of view. Creating effective publicity requires much more than expounding simple information; it always conveys value and convinces (or at least entices) its audience. To accomplish such sophisticated tasks, publicists must imagine what will interest and appeal to their audience and craft their publicity accordingly.

Being able to see things from another's point of view represents a major shift in one's thinking. Publicists must both empathize with their intended audience by anticipating how they will respond to what they see and experience, and think objectively and analytically about the show itself. Empathy for an audience requires creative imagination, while producing effective copy demands clear thinking and good writing skills.

Simple announcements can be made by young children, but publicity intended for the general public requires more maturity and sophistication. Teachers can point out the need to anticipate new points of view through imagination and emphasize its value in creating effective publicity. They can guide their students toward appreciating the public's point of view and the need to accommodate to it.

Publicity comprises a multifaceted array of tasks. As in the other phases of exhibiting student art, a team approach works well. The exhibition theme and installation design underlies all of the exhibition's publicity. The publicity team, therefore, must coordinate its efforts with those of the other teams. However, its members can usually begin their work as soon as the curatorial team decides on a theme.

CULTIVATING AN AUDIENCE

There is no reason to leave the public's response to chance. Art exhibitions provide many opportunities for students to write through publicity, labeling and signage, brochures, and catalogs. When students are highly motivated, as they are about their own art and their peers' opinions of it, they often attack publicity tasks with a tenacious enthusiasm not given to their regular writing assignments.

Publicity takes two forms: advertising and exposition. Advertising gets the word out to the public in advance of the show's opening. Press releases, posters, public announcements, and invitations whet the public's appetite, tease their curiosity, raise issues, and prompt discussions among potential viewers. When viewers have been "warmed up," they become more receptive. They can accept visual and aesthetic challenges more willingly and take in new experiences more easily.

Exposition attempts to explain the meaning of the art and the intention of the artists in a more discursive manner. The audience may read reviews and interviews that discuss the art in some depth before they see the show. Brochures and catalogs help viewers understand and appreciate what they are seeing once they attend the show.

Publicity adds new dimensions to the exhibition experience, as shown in the continuing scenario of Mrs. Bailey's art students:

> Ali is the curator who chose to work with the publicity team. The other publicists are Ward, Reshada, and Marie. They all met with the curators to hear about the exhibition theme and go over the brief and timetable. Although they had 3 weeks in which to work, they knew they would be busy because some of the publicity had to be disseminated before the actual opening.
>
> Ali and Ward decided to do the publicity for the exhibition; Reshada and Marie wanted to concentrate on a catalog. Ali and Ward produced fliers that they put up around the school 2 weeks before the opening. In the week before the show opened, they produced a series of cryptic announcements that they read over the public address system each morning. They added a "teaser" to each

message—that its meaning would only be revealed at the "Hidden Meanings" exhibition.

Reshada and Marie put together a brochure and catalog several pages in length. Reshada wrote an essay on Dürer's *Melencolia I*, speculating on the relation between his symbols and their possible meanings, and their own. As soon as Marie received the installation plan from the design team, she began to write a catalog listing the artists' names and titles in the same order as they would appear in the exhibition. Reshada and Marie interviewed each pair of artists whose works were arranged together in the show. They asked about what symbols the artists had created and what they meant. Then they wrote short, mysterious poems that included imagery from each pair of drawings, which they placed next to the respective artists' names and titles in the catalog. Here is one of the poems:

> Four ravens over pools of dark water,
> And branches dipping make nervous ripples;
> Scratches of patches of batches of matches,
> Line up to light up Jenny's eyes.

They hoped the poems would provide clues to help viewers discover secret meanings among the latent symbols. Reshada and Marie reproduced two dozen copies of the catalog just before the opening reception. They were a hit. They gave special copies signed by all the members of the exhibition teams and the artists to the principal and Mrs. Bailey.

ADVERTISING: ROMANCING THE SHOW

Publicity piques the public's interest and widens the potential audience for the exhibition. There are many ways to inform people about upcoming events. Posters and leaflets in high-traffic areas will communicate to the maximum number of people. Notices in the school newspaper have wide circulation and "commercials" can be given during the morning announcements. The school Web site and other Internet outlets offer many unique opportunities. If the exhibition is held in conjunction with a school event, such as a play or concert, the public needs to be informed about the show beforehand so they can look forward to it.

Like diamonds, publicity can be judged according to four C's: Content (not carets), Clarity, Color, and Cut.

- *Content*: All the pertinent information—who, what, where, when, why, and how—should be included. Remember to always acknowledge sponsors and donors in your publicity.
- *Clarity*: Publicity needs to be very clear about its intent and the information it communicates.
- *Color*: It should be well designed and attractive in order to appeal to viewers.
- *Cut*: Publicity must be well written and well edited. Write, rewrite; read, reread. Cut out whatever is unnecessary or gratuitous. Remember, it must first catch the interest of busy editors and then pass their critical scrutiny before they will consider it for their publications.

Announcements and Invitations

Announcements should be sent to "prime targets," or people who might have a special interest in the exhibition. The exhibition may be of interest to decision makers and stakeholders concerned with the issues being presented. As a courtesy, school administrators, members of the school board, and other dignitaries should regularly receive personal invitations to exhibitions and their openings. They want to know what is going on in their school and what is important to students. Moreover, every exhibition showcases the art program. Keeping administrators apprised of upcoming exhibitions and receptions encourages them to remain supportive.

Curators and exhibition designers often create an icon—a symbol, image, or motif—that runs throughout the exhibition, giving it a point of recognition and providing it with overall continuity. Publicists can use the icon in their announcements, posters, and other printed material as well. Attractive yet inexpensive announcements can feature a representative work of art or the show's icon on one side, with the exhibition information on the other. A postcard format allows room for four announcements on each sheet of paper and can be sent through the mail at the postcard postage rate. Photocopying the announcements on cover stock adds to their durability in the mail. Some announcements and invitations can be circulated through the school mail or distributed in public places to cut down on postage costs.

Press Releases

Sometimes topical themes arouse interest in the community. Depending on the scope or content of the exhibition, press releases can be sent to newspapers and radio and television stations. Mark Johnson (2003) provides the following pointers for student publicists:

The initial contact to any media (TV, radio, newspapers, magazines, etc.) is a call or e-mail to the contact person (i.e., the Arts and Entertainment editor). Introduce yourself, for whom you work (or represent), and the exhibition you are publicizing. On a personal note, remember that most professionals are very busy and may indicate little or no interest. Do not allow this to discourage you. . . .

Fax or e-mail a press release to this person. . . . Always include a cover letter reiterating the points of which you spoke on the phone. [Include:]
Your name/title—Publicity Coordinator
The name and location of your gallery
General exhibition information
Exhibition dates, reception date and time, gallery hours
Availability of tours, pre-opening for critics
Reader interest
"Angle" of story—i.e., importance to the (local) community (pp. 64–65)

See Case 4.1 in Part II for Paul Terrell Jr.'s detailed plan for exhibition publicity.

Posters

Posters announce exhibitions through eye-catching images and dramatic typography. They give the essential information—what, where, when—to draw the public to the event. Posters may be created individually or mass produced using silkscreen or other printing processes. Contemporary technology makes the design and production of posters very rapid. Computer programs such as Photoshop allow students to combine images, graphics, and text easily and efficiently. Finished designs can be generated directly from the stored image or sent immediately over the Internet. The school Web site has become the contemporary poster gallery. Students should be encouraged to create imaginative graphic designs to place online.

EXPOSITION

Exhibitions make ideal venues for aesthetic discussions and constructive art criticism. Different types of themes can prompt different forms of writing. Young children may write only a sentence or two about a specific work, while older children can compose more extensive, reflective, and personal essays. In schools where exhibitions make up part of the normal art landscape, students look forward to what is said about their art before and after it is viewed.

A newsletter is particularly helpful in communicating to parents at home in a timely fashion. A monthly art bulletin offers a schedule of upcoming exhibition themes and events as well as providing space for student interviews, apologia, and reviews. Art teachers can list what art projects and concepts each grade or class is working on. Usually a two-sided page is sufficient for a month's worth of art news. The school's Web site provides immediate access to the extended school "family" and community. Color images can accompany the text.

Reviews

Reviews of art and art criticism are quite different writing genres. Reviews can be included in school newspapers, art bulletins, and Web sites. They should project a positive tone intended to attract and inform potential viewers. Peeling back layers of perception and meaning takes considerable work. Students need regular opportunities to discuss art in order to develop the skills required to penetrate its many layers. When teaching students to write reviews, keep in mind that good reviews are first and foremost about the art. Even professional critics make the common mistake of writing about the art's perceived shortcomings and expressing their own opinions instead of writing about the art itself. It's very easy to say what art is not; it's much more difficult to work thoughtfully through to what it really is and what it really means. Successful reviews display an appreciation of art. The word *appreciate* means "to increase in value." When students understand that their purpose in writing reviews is to help other people enjoy as well as understand the art more, they will avoid "cheap shots," and they will not tolerate them from others. They are also more likely to value their own roles as reviewers.

At the Ross School in East Hampton, New York, students write reviews that they include in their exhibition catalogs. For an example, see Case 4.2 in Part II.

Interviews

Student interviews with peers about their art and with curators about their exhibitions extend insight and appreciation beyond the art object itself to a deeper level of meaning. Interviews allow for the exchange of ideas and points of view for both the interviewer and the person being interviewed. Interviews often shift from the art and its meaning to the artist and his or her intentions. Here, dialogue clarifies appreciation and meaning for both the interviewer and the artist.

Cross advises her students to

> first become familiar with your artist BEFORE the interview. You can do this by reading the artist's resume and other materials that [the teacher] will give you. . . . Have your questions ready. . . . Sometimes an artist will answer a question and the answer will make you think of another question—so ask it! (2003, n. p.)

She explains further:

> Prior to our visits [to artists' studios], students had explored the interview
> process with their language arts teacher. They had practiced interview tech-
> niques on teachers at the school. When they arrived at an artist's studio, they
> had a list of questions to ask; they also each recorded answers, and gave their
> answers to the one girl assigned to write about that artist. Some girls were
> assigned to take photographs of the artists in the studio. (2000, n.p.)

Cross also encouraged her students to seek direct quotes.

Another type of interview is the *apologia*, which interprets the artist's
intent as well as the art's meaning. (Our word, *apology*, comes from the
same Greek root word, *apologos*.) Apologists try to explain what the artist meant in his or her work. They defend the artist's position rather than
criticizing it or interpreting it from their own point of view. In this respect,
firsthand interviews with artists aid critical understanding immensely because they can provide insights that are not readily obvious in the artwork
itself.

Jennifer Cross has her students at the Ross School in East Hampton,
New York, interview professional artists who are represented in their shows.
The interviews are apologia; they elaborate on the artists' ideas and intent.
For a more complete description, see Case 4.3 in Part II.

Artists' Statements

Artists often appreciate an opportunity to explain what inspired their art.
Artists' statements give them a chance to sort through their ideas, reasons,
feelings, insights, and opinions. These short statements—usually less than
a page in length—can be included in brochures or installed as wall text in
the exhibition itself. Artists' statements let students reflect on their own
work, consider how others might see it, and what they might want to know
about it and the artist. Artists' statements also require students to refine
their writing through several drafts, from their most immediate, scattered
impressions to an articulate, yet compelling, paragraph or two. Teachers
can prompt students to write in different formats—descriptive, expressive,
poetic, dramatic, reflective, or rhetorical—in order to select a writing style
that matches the artistic style of the work, as well as refine their own writing style.

Artists' statements should be consistent with the thematic type and installation style of the show. If the thematic type is emotive, the artists' statements should reflect the artists' feelings. If the installation style is interactive
and calls for the viewer to play an active role, the artists' statements should

draw out the viewer by asking questions and evoking responses. Artists' statements make good writing exercises because they require students to write within a selected format and toward a specific goal. Even though their writings let students elaborate on their own thoughts and feelings, they must keep their readers foremost in their minds as well.

Diana Hampe (2003), a teacher in the Walpole High School, in Walpole, Massachusetts, gives her students three prompts and requires them to support each prompt with three statements:

1. What is the content? What is your [art] about?
2. Why are you exploring this content? Why is it meaningful to you?
3. What visual metaphors did you create to visualize your ideas and how are you using the elements of art and principles of design to say it?

Students can begin to write brief artists' statements of a sentence or two when they accession their work. Their length and variety can build over time. Eventually one student may be asked to write an artist's statement for another student, producing a rudimentary apologia. These apologia can easily grow into critiques and then reviews. They tend to remain positive because their format is based on artists' meaningful personal statements.

Brochures and Programs

Brochures and programs present the exhibition theme in a concise manner. Brochures contain short descriptions of an exhibition and the art it contains. They are intended to immediately motivate and orientate viewers upon their entering the site of the show. Here is the ideal place to outline the exhibition's theme and insert artists' statements. Including images of the artwork, the artists, or the motif of the show make them more attractive. Because of their brevity (usually one page or a double-sided sheet), they must be both terse in text and well crafted in design.

Writing a brochure requires a thorough understanding of the exhibition theme, the intent of the artworks, and the ability to get the point across clearly and succinctly. If the students are going to produce a brochure, they should decide on this early in the exhibition process and prepare drafts as the exhibition process unfolds. Brochures that are produced as an afterthought may lack freshness.

Programs reflect specific events, such as the opening reception. They list the ingredients of the event, including speakers, musicians, and any other special activities. Sponsors and patrons should be acknowledged and thanked in the program. Irvine (1997) suggests that "programs of exhibits should always include the principal, superintendent, and school board names" (p. 1).

Catalogs

Catalogs list all the works in the show, providing title, artist, medium, dimensions of the work, and other pertinent information. Catalogs can be simple or elaborate undertakings, depending on the students' abilities and the teacher's resources. Simple catalogs can be easily compiled from the accession documents accompanying each work included in the exhibition. More complex catalogs, modeled on the glossy publications produced by museums for their major shows, may contain essays about the exhibition theme written by the curators or invited authorities, information about historical influences or inspirations, biographies of the artists, or descriptive commentaries of the exhibition's development itself. Reproductions of some of the exhibited works (especially if they are in color) add an impressive feature to the catalog. Photocopy technology can produce attractive, full-color catalogs in editions of any number.

Attractive catalogs make great souvenirs for sponsors or can be sold for a profit. Students may have to seek sponsors or donors to offset the initial costs of producing catalogs. The sponsors should be prominently acknowledged and thanked in the catalog and at receptions.

Catalogs should be available at the opening and during the run of the exhibition. Ideally, they will become a permanent record of the exhibition and an example of authentic assessment for the students. However, if only one or a few can be produced, they should be returned by the viewers when they leave the show.

At the Ross School in East Hampton, New York, Jennifer Cross's students create beautiful, full-color catalogs for their exhibitions. Case 4.4 in Part II details their work.

CONCLUSION

Make no mistake, writing is a high priority in every American school. When students have opportunities to write about subjects they know well and care about deeply, and when they know their writing will be read by their peers or possibly published, they will make concerted efforts to write well and purposefully.

Exhibitions provide a wide range of writing tasks requiring an equally wide variety of writing styles. Students may use journalistic formats for newspapers and publicity blurbs. They may need to write descriptively for brochures and catalogs. Their apologia and reviews may be embellished with poetic flourishes to bring out the tenor of their subject. Yet their writing will be critically examined; it must be clear and concise, because they are writing not just for themselves but for a real audience.

Publicity asks students to go beyond their own point of view. They must foresee the perspectives of other people—other student-artists, their readers, and the people who will attend the exhibition. Interviews require students to plan for the questions they are going to ask. They must anticipate what the artist will say as well as what will be of interest to their readers.

CHAPTER 5

Exhibition Events
and Assessment

A reception is a special event that brings people together for the purpose of viewing art. This event is the culmination of a complex series of efforts involved in developing a meaningful theme, selecting art for display, designing the exhibition, installing the art in an attractive manner, and publicizing the show effectively. The reception realizes the expectations of the artists and the curators while also satisfying the aesthetic appetite of the viewing public.

Effective art exhibition accomplishes more than simply displaying works of art. It attracts viewers, informs them, and ultimately influences them in a positive manner. Ideally, viewers accept the exhibition's theme either consciously or unconsciously through the inducements made by the art and the publicity. In this respect, a positive tone always persuades more effectively, whether the artists and curators wish to present a fresh point of view, heighten awareness, or change public opinion about an important issue. Even when the theme aims at instilling beauty within the hearts of its audience, the intent must reach beyond the art itself to plumb their feelings.

THE RECEPTION

Many factors come together during an opening event. As James Gardner, the eminent exhibition designer, observed, "An exhibition does not in fact exist until it is crowded with people, and what really matters is how these people react to what they see" (Gardner & Heller, 1960, p. 5). The "people" include those involved in mounting the exhibition as well as the viewing public. McLean (1993) goes even further:

> Receptions serve a number of purposes and are an important element of the exhibition development process. Clearly, receptions draw attention to the exhibition and allow the museum to publicize its existence. . . . A less obvious but important function of reception is to provide a catharsis for project team members and other people who have worked on the exhibition. (p. 64)

On first appearance a reception may seem to be a simple gathering to view art. Unfortunately, when people mill around aimlessly, not knowing what to say or how to act, the event may prove anticlimactic. Indeed, when the public is *trained* in how to act in an exhibition, they will have a better and more aesthetic experience. Their training can be formal; their teacher can inform them of what is appropriate behavior in a gallery or museum setting, and have them rehearse it. Their training can also be informal, when they are induced to behave in certain ways and have certain experiences because they encounter people who engage them in interesting conversations about the art or entice them into activities that draw out their aesthetic responses.

A reception can have many facets, but to be successful it requires the planning and participation of many people. As in the other phases of exhibition development, a team devoted to orchestrating the reception can add greatly to the success of the exhibition.

Initially, viewers may arrive at an exhibition feeling emotions ranging from excitement to anticipation to indifference. The reception, therefore, needs to create a climate that is at once visually appealing and mentally and emotionally stimulating. Once aroused, the viewers' perception will ripen from glance to gaze, from looking to seeing, from inquiry to insight. Ideally, they can then progress to grasping the theme and fully appreciating the art. They can be influenced by what people around them say and do. In particular, curators, docents, and others who are already knowledgeable about the show can guide viewers' perceptions and attitudes.

Students should be encouraged to visit shows more than once. Art appears quite differently in the hurly-burly of a reception from when one leisurely contemplates it while alone in the gallery. Viewers may note how their own states of mind affect their perception of art on different occasions.

In Case 5.1 in Part II Deborah Diffily tells how her kindergarten class planned an exhibition that culminated in an opening event.

The Role of Docents: Informing the Public

The ambience of the reception can be greatly enhanced by those who directly engage the viewers. Unfortunately, unless curators and others involved in mounting the show are prepared to interact with the public, they may cling shyly to the sidelines during the reception. Docents, by contrast, can be trained to play an active role in creating an exciting, inquisitive, aesthetic climate by welcoming viewers, answering their questions, and even prompting their curiosity with questions of their own. In this respect, everyone involved in mounting the show should become a docent.

In museums, docents serve as guides for specific groups. In school settings, they are free to move from person to person in a more casual manner, directing attention to different works, providing information, and posing interesting questions.

The key quality of docents is that they have prepared beforehand on how to interact with viewers. They understand the exhibition theme and can articulate it clearly. They imagine how viewers will react when they see the show, and they plan their roles accordingly. They rehearse what they will say. They prepare interesting questions and specific talking points. Student-docents have an understanding of the whole show, not only of their own works.

Amenities: Music and Refreshments

Students enjoy music and refreshments at receptions because these add to the "party atmosphere." Most children and adolescents know very well how to organize a party, and they will quickly volunteer for this duty. Music, food, and speakers require additional preparation, and the noise and traffic problems they generate need to be considered. Costumes can elaborate on the exhibition's theme. If the reception is outside regular school hours or in a venue such as the cafeteria, the problems should be manageable. Specific people need to be responsible for preparing and serving food and cleaning it up when the opening is over.

Opening Program

The art teacher or a principal may officiate at the reception, or a featured dignitary from the community may elaborate on the theme and its background. Students themselves may wish to make statements or present vignettes related to the exhibition. At the reception, sponsors and donors should be publicly thanked for their help.

When the students' art is inspired by a visiting artist or an artist in the community, that person may be asked to speak. The comments of such artists often give insight into the art and help viewers to understand it more deeply. Guest speakers who can expand upon any historical background related to the theme or tell of their own experiences add to the context.

Storytellers are a wonderful resource at a reception, particularly for younger viewers. Parents, grandparents, older siblings, and members of the community may be willing to be recruited. Professional and amateur storytellers will delight both children and adults with folktales and anecdotes related to the theme. The students themselves may write, tell, or perform their own stories to unfold other dimensions of their art and their exhibition. Anthologies of folktales and stories from virtually every culture offer a ready source for material.

Students may be drawn more deeply into their viewing experience by becoming storytellers themselves:

> The Toledo Museum of Art held a story-writing contest which focused on the theme of the family dinner in African-American culture. High school students were encouraged to submit entries which referred to their own or imagined experiences, and to view the museum's newly acquired collage, "The Family Dinner," by African-American artist Romare Bearden. Prize-winners read and performed their entries at a special event celebrating the acquisition of this work of art. (Matthias & Walton, 1997, p. 1)

Performance Art

Performance art is a contemporary genre in which the event itself is a work of art. Usually the artists themselves are the main performers, but they may call upon friends for rehearsed parts or even unsuspecting members of the audience, with dramatic and spontaneous results. Performance art can take many forms, including skits, dramatic readings, tableaux, parades, celebrations, and rituals. Costumes, props, and music add excitement to the performance.

Performance art can contribute to the ambience of a show. For example, at the opening reception of sumi-e paintings inspired by Japanese scroll paintings, visitors may view a tea ceremony or even participate in one.

Photographic and Video Documentation

Visual documentation of the reception reinforces exhibiting art as a unique and important aspect of art education. Photographs made during the staging phases, as well as the final installation, will show how the exhibition was developed. Digital photographs can easily be electronically scanned for publicity purposes. A photographic record also provides students with documentation for their portfolios, contributes to authentic assessment, and represents the exhibition dramatically for publicity and advocacy purposes.

During the reception, photographic and video documentation should be made by one or more students specifically in charge of recording the event. Video, in particular, allows viewer responses to be recorded and captures the ambience of the reception. Students enjoy seeing these videotapes after the event. They can also be used to model future docent dialogues and aesthetic discussions.

Planning what will happen during the opening reception should not be left to chance. The reception is an aesthetic event in which the public first encounters new works of art. It is also a social event where people meet their friends. The task of the reception team is to facilitate both kinds of encounters in ways that lead toward aesthetic experiences.

The reception team for the *Hidden Meanings* exhibition planned what they would say and do in detail, as the scenario continues:

> Donald is the student-curator on the reception team. The other members of the reception team are Timeka, Missy, and Philip. Although their efforts would only be realized during the reception, they worked closely with the other teams because what happens at the reception needs to complement every other aspect of the exhibition's planning. They reviewed the main features of the exhibition. Donald noted, "The theme is called 'Hidden Meanings.' The idea is that these drawings are more than meets the eye, more than what you see. They have symbols in them that you have to figure out in order to understand what they really mean."
>
> "That's why the design team put them together in pairs," Timeka said, "so people will ask, 'Why are these two drawings together?' and then, maybe they will see that there are symbols in them."
>
> "The publicity team is playing up that part of it," Missy observed. "They are trying to make people curious about our exhibition by making it a mystery. I think a lot of people will show up just because they're curious."
>
> "Have Reshada or Marie asked you about your drawing yet?" Phillip asked. "They're writing really bizarre poems about each one for the catalog."
>
> "So," Donald queried, "what are we going to do to follow through on all these things?"
>
> "We could dress up and do really strange things during the reception. We could have weird music," Missy suggested. Phillip, a rather shy boy, didn't think that was a good idea.
>
> Donald observed, "We [the curators] are afraid people will just look at the pictures but not see that there are really symbols with other meanings there. That's why we put them in pairs—to make them contrast more."
>
> "I agree," Timeka said. "We should be more subtle."
>
> "We could stand near the drawings and point out the symbols and what they mean," Phillip suggested.
>
> "But symbols don't mean the same thing to everybody. Different people can think they mean different things and still be right," Timeka answered.
>
> "We could ask questions," Donald said, "like, 'I wonder why he put a snake inside that bottle?' Then, whoever is standing there will see it, but have to figure it out for himself."

The group liked that strategy. They began to develop a list of two or three questions for each drawing. They created a separate list of questions that compared pairs of drawings. They realized that they would have to rehearse the questions until they could carry on a conversation about each pair of drawings with a casual viewer.

Missy said, "There are nine pairs of drawings. Four of us can't handle all of them, especially when a couple of us are working on refreshments." The other members of the reception team immediately saw the problem. "And we don't want to just stand in front of one pair of drawings and ask the same questions; that will be pretty obvious."

The reception team decided to recruit students from the other exhibition teams and train them in their questioning strategy. Six other students joined them as incognito docents. They rehearsed conversations for several pairs of drawings so they could move around among them inconspicuously.

MAINTAINING THE EXHIBITION

Most exhibitions stay up from a few days to a few weeks. The longer the exhibition is up, the more wear and tear it will suffer. Artwork may tilt or fall. Signage may be smudged. Every exhibition needs to be well maintained throughout its entire tenure. After the reception, students who worked enthusiastically curating, designing, and installing the show often lose interest in caring for their exhibitions. Specific students should be assigned to survey the show each day and make any necessary repairs. Sabol (1997) recalls one experience:

> [Another] group of students played an important role in the operation of the Children's Art Gallery. This group of 15 students was responsible for opening and closing the gallery each day. They greeted visitors, introduced exhibits, operated video and audio tape systems, provided programs and exhibit catalogues to visitors, gave teachers packets of educational resources, kept attendance figures, demonstrated processes used by artists, monitored student behaviors, and cleaned the gallery after each group of students left. This group of students provided the public image for the gallery. (p. 12)

Some shows are intentionally short-lived. A show supporting a specific event, such as a parent-teacher organization meeting, might last little longer than the event. Many districtwide shows for Youth Art Month last only a weekend. Other exhibitions remain up for several weeks. In general, one week provides most people within the school community with ample opportunities to enjoy the exhibition. It also allows for a regular exhibition schedule with installation and dismantling time included on alternating weeks.

A maintenance checklist helps the maintenance crew. It lists everything they should attend to and provides a daily record of who did the work. Any damage can be noted as well.

AFTERMATH: DISMANTLING THE SHOW

Dismantling a show is part of the exhibition process. Students, not the art teacher, should do it. It takes more time than one might expect, and it should be well planned. A definite time and date for this final activity needs to be included in the original brief and timetable. Although it is a boring chore for teachers, children are generally quite willing to do it, because anyone can do it well. There is a sense of accomplishment and closure associated with "striking a show," especially if the teacher effusively praises a well-done job.

Artwork needs to be returned to the art teacher or the artists. The accession forms attached to the artwork facilitate this task immensely. Sometimes students rush through this duty, and artwork is damaged. Taking care to protect the artwork and to maintain the site constitute important duties, and they should be taken seriously. School administrators and janitors do not appreciate disheveled hallways and public areas. The site must also be returned to its original state.

Dismantling the show is a major undertaking when art has been borrowed from museums or exchanged with other schools. The moving of art in and out of the exhibition area, known as *drayage*, demands the utmost care. Each work must be properly packed for shipping.

EXHIBITION AS AUTHENTIC ASSESSMENT

Authentic assessment asks students to demonstrate their learning in ways that are most appropriate for them and for the nature of their learning. It breaks away from traditional modes of assessment, such as testing for right answers and solving preconceived problems. When students show what they know directly rather than simply indicating their knowledge through inferences, their ability to convey their understanding is likely to be greater, and their teacher's ability to assess the quality and extent of their knowledge is also more likely to be accurate.

Exhibiting epitomizes authentic assessment in art. Done well, exhibitions organize what students have learned and created in a deliberate manner that can be experienced and appreciated, as well as understood, by other people. The students' learning becomes apparent through their ability to convey meaning effectively to other people. Exhibitions require students to reflect on their learning, conceive it in general thematic terms, organize and present their concept as well as their art in a convincing fashion, support it with persuasive speech and writing, and field viewers' questions and responses about their art.

From a constructivist standpoint, students are expected to learn from one another in small groups and then report their findings back to the entire group. Their presentations should be substantive and accurate in their content, relevant and useful to everyone in the class, and persuasive in their argument. Teachers can surmise from the efficacy of their exhibition what they have learned and where they should go next in their education. Exhibitions fulfill these expectations handsomely.

ASSESSING THE EXHIBITION

Assessment occurs on many levels during the reception. This is the first time everyone, including the curators, sees the complete show. The people who curated the show will closely watch the reactions of visitors to the show and sometimes poll them with questionnaires. Teachers can take this opportunity to evaluate the installation, the art, the students, and the public's responses.

Assessment is the last step in the exhibition process. Museums place considerable emphasis on feedback from their audiences on many aspects of the show, including the thematic concept, the selection of works, the clarity of the supporting text, the installation of the show, and the publicity advertising it. They encourage viewers, students, and teachers to assess the efficacy of the exhibition. Was it stimulating? attractive? informative? This information is vital in helping the museum staff to create better, more appealing, more educational exhibitions in the future.

Teachers continually assess as well, whether in the form of homework, tests, discussions, or observations. Feedback to the teachers and the students who mounted the exhibitions reflects on the efficacy of the show as well as their own performance. Assessment, therefore, can occur at several different levels, taking into the account the exhibition itself, the exhibition process, the students' performance, and the effectiveness of exhibition as it relates to the art education curriculum.

Case 5.2 in Part II shows how the assessment of student learning is woven throughout the art exhibition process by Tammy McGraw at Franklin County Middle School, Franklin County, Virginia.

Viewer Feedback

Viewer feedback is the primary source of assessment information. It is important to know what viewers think of the exhibition conceptually and aesthetically. For an informal exhibition (without a formal reception), a class discussion or comments from other classes might serve as viewer feedback.

Art teachers may wish to give their students a thought-provoking question to prompt them to write a couple of sentences about what they see or how they feel. These comments can be the basis for art criticism discussions as well as for assessment.

Viewers at formal receptions might fill out "comment cards." Specific headings will point the viewers toward aspects of the exhibition requiring assessment. Irvine (1999) envisions a "'student assessment team,' with badges and tape recorders, who interview those attending [a reception] using protocol questions we have developed with the students" (p. 1).

Sabol (1997) suggests that resource materials can be developed that will help teachers ascertain what their students learned through visiting an exhibition:

> To expand learning experiences further, the [Gallery] Steering Committee created resource materials that could be used by . . . teachers after their [class visits] to the gallery. Questionnaires about vocabulary, artists, media and other exhibit content, worksheets with crossword puzzles, word searches, matching games, and word shape puzzles, interdisciplinary activities related to mathematics, science, social studies, language arts, music, and art, and bibliographies for further student research were included. Different versions of such materials were created to match the educational needs and abilities of kindergarten through sixth grade students. (p. 11)

Assessing the Process

The students directly involved in the exhibition should themselves reflect on the entire exhibition process. The exhibition brief provides a clear outline of points to consider, but the real questions are, What was effective or problematic about each step in the process? and, How did the students deal with them? More specific questions might be framed this way:

- What was most exciting and rewarding?
- What was most interesting?
- How helpful was the exhibition plan/brief?
- Was the timetable realistic?
- What difficulties or problems occurred?
- How were they handled?
- What should we have done differently?
- What should we do differently next time?
- Were people able to work together effectively?

Assessing the Students

Exhibitions are complex affairs. It is presumptuous for one or two people to claim credit for the success of an exhibition unless it was mounted by only that person or those people. Assessing individual student performance can be difficult. Two strategies offer possibilities.

The first is self-assessment. Students can evaluate their own contribution to and its effectiveness in specific parts of the process. This can be especially helpful for both students and teachers if students keep a log of their progress. The log can amend the brief that laid out the original plan for the exhibition. In this way, items that might be forgotten in the final analysis can be checked off systematically as students update their personal log. Moreover, they can rely more on the planning brief as a reference because it guides their own assessment. When teachers show daily interest in the students' log notations, students will make a greater effort to report their performance, stay on task, and remain on schedule. Even with young children, it is a good idea to review the steps involved in the exhibition process after the exhibition is hung, so children will be prepared to assess themselves in similar ways when they are older.

The second strategy involves assessing the group as a whole. Again, a checklist or a rubric gives a comprehensive overview of all aspects of the process and allows the art teacher (or the students, if they are self-assessing) to address each step in turn (see Figure 5.1).

Diego Sanchez, who teaches in Richmond, Virginia, suggests a video portfolio as a means of authentic assessment. The video format can be expanded to embrace the entire exhibition process. Students can make a video record of the entire process: debating the initial ideas leading to a theme, selecting works, discussing and installing the show, creating the publicity, and documenting the reception the video can also include the reactions of patrons viewing the show. A final "debriefing" in which the students take stock of their own work on the exhibition caps the video document (Sanchez, personal conversation, July 4, 2003).

Figure 5.1. An Assessment Rubric

	Excellent	*Satisfactory*	*Needs Work*
Assignments (Self and Committees)	Fulfilled all assignments enthusiastically; lots of ideas and initiative.	Fulfilled most assignments well and on time	Some assignments incomplete, lacking, or late
Working with Other People	Positive; works with others cheerfully; shows leadership	Cooperative, collegial, contributing	Headstrong, uncooperative,
Effort	Very strong effort; lots of effort and energy	Steady work; some initiative	Only did what told to do; little effort

Using Assessment to Modify
the Exhibition Curriculum

Assessment provides valuable information that can help teachers to modify their own exhibition and art education curricula. The feedback from viewers indicates the strengths and weaknesses of the conceptual and aesthetic features of the exhibitions. When the public has experienced a thematically well-grounded exhibition presented through a stimulating installation, they can easily report their experiences and insights. As audience appreciation grows, themes and designs will develop in sophistication. However, art teachers must have feedback to gauge their students' readiness. They also need to closely monitor the level of practical skills and conceptual insights that students acquire before the latter can proceed to the next higher step.

Assessing exhibitions serves as a bellwether for the art education curriculum as a whole. Teachers usually select for exhibition art that is attractive and has been successful for most of the students in a class. They avoid projects that are technically weak or where overall creativity is lacking. In this way they present an attractive overview of the art education program to students, teachers, parents, and administrators alike.

We take a last look at the students from Mrs. Bailey's art class as the *Hidden Meanings* exhibition opens:

> At the reception, the incognito docents made certain that they had copies of the exhibition catalog, so they could muse about the poems as well as ask questions and prompt responses from friends they met.
>
> Timeka handed out assessment cards that asked viewers to comment on the show. The reception team had worked as a group to develop the cards. They kept their questions simple:
>
> - What is the most interesting thing about this exhibition?
> - Why do you think the drawings are grouped in pairs?
> - What do you think the art means?
> - What did you discover?
>
> Donald and Phillip took turns videotaping the opening reception. They made a point of overhearing (and recording) conversations between the incognito docents who asked leading questions and viewers who were prompted to respond. The docents were very successful in their intrigue—they themselves appeared simply to be interested viewers, but they were able to engage many other people in perceptive conversations.

CONCLUSION

Receptions are social events. In this respect, students love them and want to make the most of them. However, the party atmosphere can mask the true intention of a reception: to create a genuine aesthetic experience for the viewing public. Accomplishing this goal requires a great deal of logistical planning as well as practice for social interaction. Each installation strives for an ambiance conducive to the exhibition's theme. The reception extends that mood through amenities such as refreshments and entertainment and through dialogue between viewers, artists, curators, and invited dignitaries.

Exhibition completes one artistic cycle while anticipating a creative overture to follow. Exhibition feedback from viewers and students provides a wellspring for motivation and new ideas for future art projects.

Assessment can guide the development of an exhibition program over time. By reflecting on strengths and weaknesses, students and teachers can refine each phase of the process and make it more sophisticated. Assessments can be conducted by many parties, including the students who worked on the show, the viewing public, and the teacher. Each group provides a unique perspective.

CHAPTER 6

Teaching Art Exhibition

Teachers often take the task of exhibiting entirely upon themselves. They may feel that it poses too great an effort for their students or that such a task is outside the scope of the art curriculum. However, for students to learn most effectively, they need to do their own work. When students produce their own exhibitions, as Karen Robben, an art teacher in Salina, Kansas, points out, "They learn how much planning and preparation is involved in presenting a professional show, and more importantly, they learn to take pride in their work" (personal correspondence, 2002). The task should match their abilities. When students begin by learning simple exhibition concepts and skills, and progress slowly yet steadily to more complex projects, more ambitious exhibitions become feasible. They recognize their own actual abilities at every step. The skills and concepts involved in every phase of exhibition elaborate on the core knowledge that constitutes comprehensive art education.

Most school administrators, especially at the elementary level, expect student art to be displayed prominently and changed frequently. Many classroom teachers, as well as art teachers, spend long hours putting up and taking down displays. However, when students are not involved in the exhibition process, they cannot benefit from these experiences. If they do not have firsthand opportunities to generate themes, design and install shows, create publicity, and host receptions, they cannot really appreciate or understand how exhibitions work. Moreover, they will never develop any genuine appreciation or sophisticated insights about the purposes of exhibitions.

THE ROLE OF THE TEACHER:
FACILITATOR, SUPERVISOR, INSTRUCTOR

Teaching students to exhibit their own art and the art of others requires of teachers the same skills needed in other areas of art education. They must understand the concepts and skills inherent in exhibition. They must be able to organize them into a workable curriculum made up of lessons and units that progress from simple to complex, from general to specific, and from naive to sophisticated. Teachers must be able to articulate the concepts related to exhibiting and demonstrate them as activities. They must also express their own enthusiasm in order to motivate their students. Paige Barlow, an art teacher from Milledgeville, Georgia, observes, "As a teacher, I really try to improve the quality of their artwork because I want them to exhibit it. It also inspires me to involve new ideas in my art curriculum" (personal correspondence, 2002).

Decision making needs to be complemented with challenging yet practical plans. As the scope and scale of exhibitions widen, student responsibility should also increase, rippling outward to encompass more decisions, more components, more planning, and more venues. The students' level of responsibility should reflect their abilities, allowing them to become more independent as they mature.

As a supervisor, the art teacher sees the big picture. She can anticipate problems before they arise and steer students away from them. She can bring overly lofty student aspirations back down to earth. As a facilitator, the art teacher can expedite many situations over which students have no control. Teachers need to keep a sensitive finger on the pulse of the exhibition as it develops. Student actions should be well supervised in order to be adequately facilitated. They should check their decisions and plans with the teacher at each step. Checklists are helpful in this respect. They provide a clear structure for detail without imposing unnecessary scrutiny.

DEVELOPING AN EXHIBITION PROGRAM

Scheduling a show for every class during the school year may seem a daunting prospect for many teachers who have never done it before. It is advisable to begin with just one or two grade levels, preferably with younger children in elementary school, and with more advanced students in middle and high school. By beginning with the first and second grades, for instance, exhibitions will be simple and direct, and the students will be especially enthusiastic. As youngsters advance to the next grade, they will clamor to exhibit again—"Are we going to have another show like we did last year?"—giving the teacher an incentive to build upon their previous experience with new exhibiting ideas and inventions. Within a few years each grade will steadily progress to higher levels of ability and every grade will be exhibiting.

At the secondary level, it is advanced art students or members of the Art Club who feel most confident about the quality of their art, and they are quite willing to exhibit it. They readily grasp the concepts and themes associated with exhibiting and view exhibiting as a special opportunity. The direction is reversed here: As advanced art students learn to exhibit their own work and, later, the work of others, it becomes obvious to other art students that they could engage in this activity as well. At that point, lower-level classes can be added to the exhibition roster.

In a typical elementary school, art teachers teach between 20 and 30 classes per week. In the course of a school year, each class can produce its own one-week exhibit in the art room or on a nearby bulletin board. It is a good idea to stagger different projects and different grades throughout the school year so no sense of competition develops. An alternating schedule (K, 2, 4, 1, 3, 5, K, 2, 4, 1, 3, 5, K, 2, 4, 1, 3, 5) works very well. The same rotating strategy can be used in middle school and high school.

Exhibition schedules build gradually. Each success leads step by step to an ongoing exhibiting schedule. It may take several years before all classes exhibit on a regular basis. As teachers become more experienced and success follows success, they will gain the confidence to try a wider variety of thematic types, installation styles, and later, more varied publicity and exhibition events.

WORKING WITH AN ARTIST

One of the most interesting types of shows involves bringing a professional (or amateur) adult artist into the school and mounting an exhibition of his or her art. Artists-in-residence often have a show to celebrate their work with the students when their tenure in the school is complete. It is especially important to involve the students in the exhibition process after they have worked with the artist over an extended period of time. By acting as curators, designers, installers, and publicists for a professional artist, they realize their own sense of fulfillment and closure and better understand the artist's purpose and intention in exhibiting.

Students make a clear distinction between exhibiting their own work and exhibiting that of a professional artist. The artist's stature and reputation are unquestioned. They quickly discover that they must do much more than simply hang the works if the artist is to be genuinely understood and appreciated. Moreover, they take their roles as curators and designers very seriously.

Some teachers invite artists to exhibit at their schools, while others encourage students to make contacts. At the Ross School, Jennifer Cross (2002) makes the initial overtures to artists, but her students follow them up with interviews, biographies, and trips to the artists' studios. In many cases they select the works that will be shown in their school from the artists' personal body of work. When students have an opportunity to work with the artists, ask questions, and discuss aesthetic issues, their insights into the possibilities for exhibition deepen. (See Case 6.1 in Part II for a description of how

Carolyn Sutton and Peter Brunn at the Park School involve professional artists in their art program.)

JURIED SHOWS AND COMPETITIONS

Competition in art has a long tradition, reaching back to ancient times, when artists vied for large-scale architectural and monumental commissions. During the 18th and 19th centuries, European academies held annual salons that awarded prizes and medals for what were judged to be the best paintings and sculptures in the show. Some of the prizes, such as the Prix de Rome, were zealously sought after because they paid for several years of study abroad. Even without a monetary award, the prestige of winning a salon prize guaranteed lucrative commissions from collectors and patrons. Today many professional and amateur art societies still hold juried exhibitions, with an array of prizes awarded in numerous categories. This tradition resonates through art education, where many opportunities continue to flourish for children and adolescents to submit their art in competitive shows.

Art teachers frequently seek out competitions and encourage their students to enter them. Winning brings prestige to the students, their teachers, and their schools and sometimes engenders support for the art program from school administrators. However, if their work is not accepted, or if they don't win, both teachers and students may be deeply disappointed or interpret the rejection of their art as a personal failure. Consequently, some teachers and parents who equate showing art with competition may dismiss exhibition altogether. Teachers must clearly distinguish exhibition and its many benefits from competitions and their potential drawbacks. It is equally important to remove any competitive elements from exhibitions held within the school. Selecting art using objective criteria; involving students in all phases of the exhibition process; and avoiding prizes, honors, and winners keeps the focus on the art, where it should be. When students have frequent opportunities to exhibit, they embrace the practice with pride, enthusiasm, creativity, and excitement. The National Art Education Association (NAEA) has set rigorous guidelines for student participation in competitions (see the Appendix).

In juried exhibitions, jurors are typically professional artists, critics, or other people of supposed superior aesthetic sensibility who select the works to be exhibited. Presumably, jurors are objective and base their choices on purely professional insights. A show may have one juror; or it may have several, to enhance the aura of objectivity. In reality, jurors can be very subjective and capricious, and they may disregard the exhibition's theme, if there is one. When students do not participate in the selection process, they may feel particularly alienated and at the mercy of an unsympathetic outsider.

Moreover, they are excluded from an important step in the overall exhibition process. If jurors are used, they should thoroughly discuss with the students the show's theme and their method for selecting works. Students need to trust the jurors and feel they are working in their best interests.

One of the most sensitive issues about exhibiting student art relates to awards and prizes. Juried exhibitions emphasize the awards; thematic exhibitions emphasize the art. Competitions are juried; shows in museums and quality galleries are curated. The works that are selected best exemplify a clearly conceived theme. Competing for prizes misses the point of exhibiting art that, at its heart, strives to present art to the public in the best possible way. Awards detract from the art itself, with the implication that keeping one's eye on the prize is more important than what the art expresses, or that the public needs to be told which works are the best in order to appreciate them more. Indeed, the public enjoys drawing its own conclusions about what it sees.

ORIGINALITY

Works that are not original should be discouraged, no matter how technically proficient they may be (see the Appendix). Teachers control the exhibition schedule and therefore can coordinate shows with artistic projects that emphasize a high degree of originality, creativity, and expression and have a high rate of success within the class as a whole.

Postmodernism poses a potential problem for the traditional idea of originality in art. Postmodern theory encourages appropriating images indiscriminately from other artists, arguing that once an image enters the visual culture, it is fair game for artists. Contemporary reproduction methods and graphic software programs make virtually any image in a book or on the Internet extremely easy to download, copy, and use.

Aestheticians continue to split hairs over how much an artist can "borrow" from the works of other artists and still claim it as their own. However, many teachers still maintain that student art, and especially student art that is exhibited, should be entirely original. Students should disclose the source of their images, how they have used them, and their intentions and meanings. Advanced Placement (AP) maintains strict guidelines regarding originality in student artwork.

CONTROVERSIAL ART

Controversial art falls into two categories: offensive art and confrontational art. Offensive art usually offends through the content of the artwork itself.

Confrontational art, by contrast, reflects the provocative intention of the artist or the curator.

Offensive Art

A school is a public institution with the specific mission of educating children in a physically and psychologically safe and protective environment. While there are many options for expression and exhibition, the thresholds for safety and protection are absolute. Schools are conservative by nature. Parents and guardians know that their children are immature, impressionable, vulnerable, sensitive, and can be easily hurt. Parents and guardians want their children to be physically, emotionally, and mentally safe while they are in school. They therefore expect teachers, other students, and participants in the school environment as a whole to strive only for the best interests and welfare of their children.

Schools are compulsory; children must attend them. Students are inevitably exposed to everything that is there. They cannot choose what to see or avoid, as they might a public concert or a motion picture. Schools therefore have an ethical obligation to curtail what may be potentially offensive to students.

Most schools have stated policies or published codes for behavior, dress, and language. Students and teachers are expected to be tolerant in matters of race, religion, and creed. They are expected to be patient with other individuals' mental, emotional, and physical limitations. Most school codes explicitly prohibit any direct and indirect references to violence, crime, weapons, drugs, tobacco, alcohol, or sex. Certain visual symbols, including graffiti, tags, or even gang colors, are generally forbidden. In addition, as public institutions, the schools themselves must be physically safe and must comply with fire, safety, and health codes. For the most part, students and teachers understand the social, safety, and civil motives underlying these codes, and they comply with them willingly.

Curiously, these "rules" are malleable, contingent on various factors. In most schools, for example, the image of a gun would not be acceptable in a student's drawing; however, if a slashed circle is superimposed over it so that it symbolically reads "no guns," it might be allowed. Further, guns shown in a historical context, such as a painting depicting a Civil War battle, would probably pass muster. The symbolic nature of art makes it open to interpretation on many levels. What may be offensive to one person may be innocuous to another.

Imagery or symbols that might be quite acceptable in a local museum or public gallery may cross the line in a school. Nudity is an obvious example. The sexual and pornographic baggage associated with nudity makes it taboo. As often as not, violations of school codes are inadvertent or insensitive rather than malicious. However, students do sometimes intentionally test the limits with offensive art.

Confrontational Art

Occasionally, the desire to provoke the viewer or test the limits of propriety may drive the theme and the installation into the realm of confrontational art. The motivations of the artist or curator generally fall under four characterizations: "shock schlock," "the cheap shot," "feel my pain," and "challenging boundaries." All these motivations have long traditions in the adult art world.

"Shock schlock" asserts that the merit of the art rests on the daring of the artist to break convention—"I can get away with this because I dare to." While such art may initially attract attention, it is most likely egotistical and unlikely to demonstrate an important idea or influence people in a positive way. Brashness and bravado do not substitute for creativity or curatorial wisdom.

Likewise, the "cheap shot" requires only a minimum of creative effort. An installation of a pile of leaves, for example, is simply the lazy artist's oblique and expedient solution to a misinterpreted assignment. The student may profess an elaborate rationale, but it is likely to ring hollow.

When students produce work described as "feel my pain," their feelings may be genuine. Sometimes students are legitimately upset by painful personal experiences (the death of a friend), compelling social issues (abortion), or tragic world events (9/11). They may feel a great deal of pain or outrage and think the best way to convey their own feelings is to evoke them in others. However, *incite* does not equate with *insight*. In an exhibition setting where emotions are meant to be controlled, people are repulsed by overt expressions of pain and rage, just as they do not enjoy watching a child throw a temper tantrum in a public place. Viewers are more easily convinced by a persuasive, positive appeal than by a hysterical scream.

The fourth characterization, "challenging boundaries," is more problematic in art. Western artists have traditionally pursued innovative change as one of their most cherished ideals. They aspire to be avant-garde, to be visionaries who are ahead of everyone else. However, the unfortunate outcome in public schools may be to condemn the student, the teacher, or the art program for a work of art that is too radical for a school setting, rather than examining its underlying idea. Students need to understand the consequences of their expressions, especially when they choose to exhibit them. Teachers should rein in potentially controversial works before they are exhibited by discussing the possible reactions that people will have to them. Artists and curators require better reasons for exhibiting than that of simply exciting public sentiment.

Postmodernism, with its professed agenda of social reconstruction, encourages challenging the status quo. Postmodern art goes to considerable lengths to be edgy and "in your face." Consequently, there is the potential for confrontation between postmodern aesthetics and conservative public school traditions. Teachers will have to sort this out within the contexts of their own curricula, schools, and communities.

Thoughtful planning and preparation for exhibitions can generally avoid both these types of controversy before they occur. Several parameters ensure successful shows:

- *Know your community.* Teachers need to be aware of the traditions and standards of their communities and to be alert to the expectations of parents, school administrators, and the school board. Keep these in mind while selecting themes and art.
- *Keep it positive.* Art exhibition themes represent important ideas intended to influence viewers in a positive way. This is a guiding principle and should be taught early and repeated often. Positively influencing the public should never be sacrificed for attracting attention.
- *Emphasize that the exhibition theme guides everything else.* Criteria for selecting works of art stem from the theme, as does the installation design and publicity. While it is not necessary to write exclusionary descriptors into the criteria, curators should clearly understand that their decisions must comply with school standards and with safety, fire, and health codes.
- *Recognize that exhibitions are social events.* Students should be made aware of the social dynamics coursing through exhibitions. They should strive to promote positive social interaction from curators, docents, and artists. Sarcasm, ridicule, or other provocative speech, actions, or text have no place in a well-planned exhibition. Encourage common sense and common decency.
- *Know your curators.* Sometimes students make mistakes because they don't know what to do. If they are overwhelmed by a show that is too big for them, they might revert to an expedient solution. Select responsible people for the most responsible jobs.
- *Stay on top of the process.* Supervise each phase of the exhibition process. Break the exhibition brief down into easily accomplished tasks and have students and teams sign off on them as they complete them. Require brief oral or written reports at key points during the exhibition's development. The teacher can avert many problems as well as controversies by closely overseeing the emerging enterprise.
- *Ameliorate problems.* If a controversy arises, don't overreact. That may be exactly what the student wants. Instead, deal with it as an aesthetic problem, discuss it with the individual or the whole exhibition

team, and resolve the issue before the artwork is installed. Students should understand that art that conflicts with school policies may not be exhibited or may even be removed if someone objects.

- *Success begets success.* In most cases, especially in elementary school, the teacher picks the unit or project that will be exhibited. Wise teachers usually select art that is attractive and colorful and demonstrates a high level of achievement among most of the students. While the students may develop the theme and install the work, the show is likely to be successful because the work was successful in the first place. As students learn how exhibitions work and recognize the positive impact they have on the public, they are much more likely to seek applause than shock.

LEGAL CONSIDERATIONS

Safety Concerns and Fire Regulations

Health and safety are prime considerations in every school. Common sense dictates that anything that could possibly pose a direct or indirect threat to the welfare of children or adults in a school cannot be exhibited. Most traditional media and installation designs do not pose any danger. Some media, however, can be unsafe for some individuals. Dust, in any form, for example, can distress asthmatics. Top-heavy works must be well secured. Art made from organic matter might attract insects. Teachers need to comply with school policies regarding installations and adhere to the safety regulations prescribed by the local fire department. When these policies and regulations are presented as serving the common good, students usually follow them fastidiously.

Safety may influence the design of an installation and even the selection of certain artworks. Much art is flammable and should not be crowded together or hung within 18 inches of the ceiling. As Michael Gettings points out, "The fire marshals go nuts if you place art on the wall in one continuous fashion without any breaks" (personal correspondence, 2000). Dangling strings and streamers and hanging fabrics pose potentially dangerous problems. Exhibition designers must make sure three-dimensional works would not obstruct free passage during an emergency. Exits cannot be blocked or emergency signs obscured.

Parental Permissions

Generally, art exhibited within the school as part of the normal school routine does not require parental permission. However, parental permission is often needed when students' names, photographs, or artwork are presented outside the school, exchanged with other schools, placed on the Internet, or published. (See Figure 6.1 for a sample permission form.) If these cases are few in number they can be handled on an individual basis. If such shows are frequent, one permission covering a variety of instances can be secured at the beginning of the school year.

Security and Insurance

Many teachers fear vandalism or breakage. However, in a national survey of art teachers, less than 5% had actually experienced any willful damage or theft of student art work (Burton, 2004). Of the few reported incidents, half occurred at sites away from school, such as malls. The experience nevertheless disheartens teachers, students, and parents alike. Diane Sorchik, of Sussex, New Jersey, spoke of having art stolen as her "greatest frustration related to exhibiting student art, [even though] in 20 years, we've lost only two pieces" (personal correspondence, 2002). By exercising reasonable care and security, vandalism and theft can be minimized. It is certainly not a reason to avoid exhibiting.

Figure 6.1. Parental Permission Form

Date _____

I give permission for my child's _____ (name)

artwork to be exhibited at _____ (name of exhibition)

to be held at _____ (venue)

during _____ (dates)

The name of the school and the teacher's name will be prominently displayed.

I further give permission for my child's artwork to be labeled with his/her name.

Yes _____   No _____

I REFUSE to allow my child's artwork to be exhibited. _____

_____

Signature of Parent

Security and insurance occasionally must be considered, especially when art is borrowed from a museum or a collector. Cross (2000, n.p.) points out,

> We had a rider put on our own [school's] insurance policy to cover the value of [borrowed] works against loss or damage, but many times you can have artists sign a waiver saying they understand that, although not insured, all reasonable care will be taken to see that works will be treated in a safe and secure manner.

Ideally, the school can provide a secure location, such as a lockable gallery, for its exhibitions. The risk is minimal, and thus, the rider is usually minimal. Student work generally does not have to be insured.

DEVELOPING SUPPORT FOR EXHIBITIONS

Art Clubs and Volunteer Helpers

A student art club is a ready and reliable source of help. Club members are likely to be the most dedicated students and those who are also most interested in art and have the best technical skills and judgment. They can act as leaders or supervisors for novices. They readily see the necessity of each of the many tasks and how they must fit together to achieve a final, successful result. Carol Hilgemann, in North Pole, Alaska, noted, "In the annual Art Demonstration Night, Art Club students are totally responsible for planning, installing, and dismantling the exhibition in the school's common area" (personal correspondence, 2002).

Volunteers drawn from the ranks of parents, grandparents, and other members of the community are especially helpful in elementary school. Michael Luehrmann (2003) observes,

> Remembering the importance of family environment, communicate with parents through newsletters that let them know what children are learning in art. These efforts that mesh with the overall mission of the school will not go unnoticed by the principal. This will also help generate interest from parents and caregivers who can actively contribute to the art program as helpers or through presentations of art works and cultural information. Cultivating parents who feel strongly about the art program can provide art teachers with their strongest allies when approaching administrators for greater financial support and better conditions for teaching and learning. Parents have clout with the school (p. 2).

Mounting an exhibition frequently involves several tasks happening at once. Volunteers can work with small groups outside the classroom while the teacher continues with his or her lessons. It is important that volunteers understand that their role is to supervise and facilitate and that they should not try to take over the job themselves. Like teachers, they must exercise self-restraint and allow the children to make their own decisions so learning can occur. Adults serve an especially important role when they can carry out potentially unsafe tasks such as climbing on ladders or changing lighting.

Fund-Raising

As the scope and scale of exhibitions increase, so do their budgets. When artwork is mounted on drawing or construction paper, teachers can usually supply the needed resources from their own stores. As exhibitions become more ambitious and complex, additional resources (and money) may be needed (Burton, 2005).

Because exhibitions put forward art, students, the school, and the art program in a positive light, many people may be willing to help. Businesses, corporations, and individuals might wish to donate funds. A donation may be forthcoming when the exhibition reflects the corporate interests of the patron. Or there may be other motivations; a local architect, for example, might be delighted to sponsor an exhibition related to architecture. Companies and businesses may offer materials in kind, such as matboard, framing, or postage. Frame shops and other art-related businesses are often willing to contribute their matte scraps. A printer could be willing to produce catalogs or brochures free of charge or at cost.

Professional and community organizations, foundations, and educational agencies offer small grants for special projects, especially if they are highly visible and contribute to the community as a whole. School art organizations, such as parents' Art Booster Clubs, student Art Clubs, or NAEA Art Honor Society chapters, can raise money or gather supplies. Some schools have art sales once or twice a year or create school-related T-shirts and other items for sale.

School administrators are very sensitive to praise and other positive feedback from parents and the community at large. They may be quite willing to contribute additional funds for exhibitions as they grow in visibility. Knowing how many parents visited a show and having their written comments will help to bolster your case.

The sponsors and donors should always be thanked profusely, at receptions, in programs, and in advance publicity. Irvine (1997, p. 1) suggests that students, as well as their teachers, send letters identifying patrons as "Art Champions," acknowledging their contributions, and stating how they were used.

Selling Student Art

Adult art is generally shown in two venues: museums and galleries. Museums exhibit art that is held in public trust or borrowed from other public or private collections. People view and enjoy the art, but they cannot buy it.

Galleries, by contrast, are commercial enterprises; they offer the art they display for sale.

Generally, exhibitions of student art follow the museum model. The students retain ownership of their work and it is eventually returned to them. However, some teachers employ the gallery model and stage art sales of their students' work. The proceeds can go directly to the student; to the school or art program; or for a special purpose, such as a charity.

Teachers who wish to hold art sales of student work should be aware of the temperament of their community. While such efforts may be welcomed in some places, other communities may frown on them. Small, tight-knit communities where people know each other may work best; communities where people anxiously try "to keep up with the Joneses" should be avoided for art sales. As with all student art exhibitions, art sales should be efforts to bring people together in a positive forum. They should not be divisive. (See Case 6.2 in Part II to discover how Christa Wise, an art teacher in Saugatuck, Michigan, leases student art to people in her community to raise funds for the art program).

Art that is presented in a tacky, "school art" manner can be embarrassing to parents who do not see its aesthetic merit. Their attitudes often change when it is presented in a more professional fashion. While teachers should guard against "selling the frame" and should emphasize the artistic and aesthetic qualities of the work itself, respectable presentation can help the public see the art in its best light.

Students and their parents must both give their permission before the students' art may be sold, kept by the school for its own collection, or given as gifts. Many teachers offer parents and guardians an opportunity to purchase their child's work in advance, before the general public sees it. The work often amazes them and they are happy to buy it.

In their art auction catalogs, teachers at Maymont Elementary School in Richmond, Virginia, outlined a bidding procedure. The catalogs explained how to bid, when bidding was over, and where to pay for and pick up purchases. Each catalog was emblazoned with a large number that served as a bidding number. The school held a silent auction at which people were allowed to write their bidding number on a card next to a work of art. In this way, they could raise the bid on favorite pieces without "competing" openly (Maymont Elementary School, 1998).

Some teachers use all the profits from their sales or auctions to support their art programs, while others take just a percentage or fee to offset the costs of matting, publicity, and the reception. In other instances, students receive the full proceeds of their sales.

Students often feel that they have little influence on issues that are important to them. When their art reflects a social issue and its sale contributes to a charity representing that cause, they discover a way to assert their influence, exercise their social conscience, and satisfy their artistic expression. From the beginning, they should know about the charitable intent of the sales, and it should be clearly announced in the publicity. The project called Empty Bowls is a good example. Begun by high school art teachers in Michigan in 1990, guests were served a simple meal of soup in bowls made by students as a fund-raiser to support a food drive. The guests received their bowls for a donation. "Since then, Empty Bowls events have been held throughout the world, and millions of dollars have been raised to combat hunger" (Taylor, 2002, p. 48).

Exhibition as Advocacy for Art

Exhibiting art is a very strong advocacy tool. Exhibition "sells" a school's art program by making the public aware of its quality and vitality. It has a strong influence on everyone throughout the school—students, teachers, staff, administrators, parents and guardians, and the community in general. When administrators and parents are happy with what they see, they tend to support art programs and art teachers. As Luehrman (2003) points out:

> If they lack experience in art, many principals may feel inadequate in their ability to even discuss the subject [of art]. They may be privately embarrassed, particularly in an elementary school, if they see very young students learning art concepts that they themselves know little or nothing about, having not encountered them in their own schooling or family background. Take this into consideration and be understanding. Be careful not to project an elitist art stance that may alienate a principal whose past or lack of experience may have led to either a narrow definition of art, or "art anxiety," or even a distain for a subject that for them has never been demystified. It may take time for some principals to realize the value of a quality art program. Your patience and perseverance may be tested; there may be small increments of improvement in appreciation. Recognize that the biggest factor will likely be what your principal sees of your own dedication and enthusiasm for art and teaching.
>
> The principal's interest in and positive value judgments about the art program are likely to be most strongly influenced by the visual qualities of students' art work in school and community exhibits. Publicly visible art events that project to the community a positive image of the learning that goes on in the art program will help the teacher accumulate "capital" that can usually be redeemed for support that is needed. (pp. 1–2)

TURNING EMPTY SPACES INTO PLACES FOR ART

Every school offers its own unique opportunities for exhibition. Small-scale exhibitions generally occur in or near classrooms or the art room. As students acquire skills and conceptual strength, and as art teachers gain confidence and ambition, shows tend to reach farther—through the halls of the school, into public areas and offices, and into nooks and crannies that might be otherwise overlooked. Eventually, students (with the encouragement of their art teachers) may begin to exhibit at special events at the school and then outside the school, in their community.

Small spaces, of course, suggest small shows, or at least parts of shows. A large exhibition can spread over a considerable distance, for example, in the halls of a school. Large spaces, such as the cafeteria or school lobby, require suitable, large amounts of work to adequately make use of the space. Too few works in a cavernous space can make them ineffectual. Administrators often welcome handsome, well-presented work that projects a creative and colorful impression of the school. The work needs to be appropriate to the site, and it needs to be shown in the right place.

The Classroom/Art Room

The art room is an ideal site for exhibiting student art. In an elementary school, there are enough weeks in the school year to allow each class to have at least one weekly exhibit of its work. These exhibits can be passive—simply displayed without comment—or teachers may include them as part of an active teaching strategy. They might regularly begin each class with a few minutes' reflection on the exhibition of the week. Exhibitions in the art room send a strong message about the art teacher's intense interest in every student's art. At the secondary level, classwide, weekly exhibitions "sell" the art program to students. Seeing attractive work done by upper-level students whets the appetite of other students, encouraging them to enroll in art classes. When students perceive exhibiting as a normal outcome of the artistic process, they are easily encouraged to participate; indeed, they will expect to exhibit. Weekly exhibitions also provide an ongoing basis for rich aesthetic and art criticism discussions.

Classrooms are an ideal setting for ongoing artistic assignments that might be too extensive for the entire class to undertake at once. For example, one or two students might put up a weekly show of their photography. By extending the time frame to several months, each child in the class can exhibit several of his or her photographs, while it would not be possible for all the students to show their photographs simultaneously.

School Hallways

The bulletin boards and hallways immediately outside the art room are prime locations for exhibiting art. In elementary schools, principals expect teachers to present attractive art displays and change them regularly. Classroom teachers often decorate bulletin boards with seasonal themes, special projects, essays, and even homework. Art teachers have the special advantage of an endless supply of beautiful, creative visual art. When they involve their students in the exhibition process, both children and teachers see art in a different light and learn about it in additional ways.

Contemporary schools often are designed to showcase art and art programs by locating the art room near the main school entrance, where visitors immediately encounter it upon entering the building. Astute art teachers capitalize on the exhibition opportunities provided by such architecture to their fullest advantage.

Sherry Snowden, at Hays High School, in Buda, Texas, maximizes her exhibition space by placing "locker toppers" along the tops of the lockers that line her hallways. (See Figure 6.2 and Case 6.3 in Part II).

School Gallery

Many schools designate a separate room as an art gallery. An art gallery adds to the prestige and pride of the school and offers a specific location for full-scale exhibitions and receptions. Its presence announces that art is valued

Figure 6.2. Locker Toppers. Sherry Snowden, Hays High School, Buda, Texas. Sherry Snowden designed locker toppers to display dozens of works of art in the hallways of her school.

Photo: Sherry Snowden

and vital at that school. A gallery can expand exhibition opportunities as well. Insurable art borrowed from museums, professional artists, and collectors usually requires a room that can be securely locked.

Gallery areas may be open, such as the school lobby, or within a designated room, similar to a professional gallery. An area committed to art requires extra care and attention but invites student involvement in its content as well as its maintenance. Lighting and wall color can be more flexible, special displays that are not possible in high traffic areas can be set up, and valuable artwork can be protected. A school gallery also allows for a yearlong exhibition program in which several shows can be planned ahead.

Ralph Caouette's students organize several shows a year at the Bowes Gallery, within Wachusett Regional High School, in Holden, Massachusetts. (See Figure 6.3 and Case 6.4 in Part II for more about the Bowes Gallery).

Figure 6.3. Bowes Art Gallery, Wachusett Regional High School, Holden, Massachusetts. Ralph Caouette and his Art Club schedule 9 to 11 shows each year to present the art of students, local professional artists, and artists who are alumni of their school.

Photo: Ralph Caouette

School Events and Community Events Held at School

Special events, such as plays and concerts, provide excellent, albeit fleeting, occasions for showing art. When the art exemplifies the event, it is especially effective. For example, when the audience of a play must pass through a gauntlet of well-presented costume sketches and stage designs on the way to their seats, they will better appreciate the ingenuity and effort that has gone into the entire theatrical production. Parent-teacher-organization and other community meetings offer wonderful opportunities to present art (and the art program) to parents and influential community leaders. Graduation is a major event in students' lives that should be recognized through an art exhibition.

Anne Ezzelle teaches art at Reams Road Elementary School, in Chesterfield, Virginia. She exhibits at least one work by every child during Back-to-School Night. (Read more about her exhibition in Case 6.5 in Part II).

The lobby, cafeteria, and auditorium in a school invites art exhibitions. Most students, faculty, and visitors pass through these areas daily, making them ideal locations. Large-scale works are particularly effective in open areas, such as a cafeteria or auditorium. The main office and offices of administrators, counselors, nurses, and others provide additional excellent sites in which to hang art. Works located in offices should be well matted, or even framed, and changed regularly, to make the best possible impression on their occupants as well as on visitors.

Sites Throughout the School

Exhibiting at several sites throughout the school multiplies exhibition opportunities tremendously. More themes can be tried out, while different locations may require different installation strategies. Where a show is located within the school can even determine different audiences (by grade level in elementary schools or by subject area in secondary schools).

Working at several sites simultaneously raises serious logistical considerations. Generally students must take on more of the planning, installation, and dismantling chores, while the art teacher assumes a supervisory role.

George Szekely turns his students into "gallery owners," each with his or her own designated area in which to display his or her art and to change "shows" frequently (Case 6.6 in Part II discusses Szekely's gallery owners).

Schoolwide Shows

Annual schoolwide exhibitions are a mainstay of art education. Most schools hold elaborate fine arts exhibitions during March, which is Youth Art Month, or near the end of the school year. Many schools also hold another major fine arts festival or evening during the fall semester. Large-scale events require considerable advance planning and entail enormous amounts of work for art teachers. Often, the entire show must be put up, viewed, and taken down in a single weekend, or even in a single day. Nevertheless, this is sometimes the only opportunity during the school year for the fine arts to shine.

The complexity, extended time frame, and amount of work may dissuade some art teachers from bringing their students into the process of mounting major exhibitions. However, having students help with the tasks they are able to do makes them aware of the amount of effort that goes into it, teaches them valuable technical and social skills, extends their conception of the time frame needed to produce a major event, and allows them to savor the praise of their peers, parents, teachers, and the community at large. When they have opportunities to be involved over several years, their knowledge and skills accumulate and makes them even more capable. Interested, trusted students may also work with more advanced classes to help them "learn the ropes" for the next year.

Districtwide or Regional Shows

Districtwide shows are a fixture in art education programs, whether they celebrate Youth Art Month in March, close the school year with a fine arts festival, or are held at some other time. Art supervisors seize the opportunity to present the collective achievements of all their art programs to the entire community at one magnificent finale. Districtwide shows present art and art education to the maximum number of parents, guardians, and relatives, through a dazzling array of art. Through coordination with their art supervisor or a designated team, art teachers from across the district combine their efforts to present an art extravaganza that will attract the whole community. Districtwide shows are generally held in a centrally located school, a community center, or a shopping mall; as many students as possible are represented. In many cases, at least one work from each student is displayed, which entails considerable efforts in organization and logistics.

Teachers who mount districtwide and regional shows agree that planning is essential and should begin as early as possible. Ilona Wale (1999), in Cave Creek, Arizona, recommends setting aside artwork from the beginning of the year, checking students off on a checklist so everyone is eventually represented, and ensuring that a wide variety of art is selected. Wale requires at least 2 months of planning and organizing to realize her Art Fair in May. She recruits volunteers and students early in April and meets with them to decide on hands-on activities and to write labels. The Art Fair is publicized one month prior to its opening, with fliers sent home with each student 2 weeks, 1 week, and 1 or 2 days before it opens. Personal invitations go to district administrators and governing board members. Things move into high gear the week before the opening. Volunteers label and mount the work, prepare refreshments, and hang the show the day of the Art Fair.

Many exhibitions, large and small, must be squeezed into a busy school or community schedule and therefore have a very short tenure, of a day or perhaps a weekend. Hanging the show and holding a reception often must happen within an equally constricted time frame, demanding efficient planning and execution. Dismantling the show must be handled with equal aplomb and efficiency (Wale, 1999).

Between Schools

Exchanges of art between schools excite everyone. Students are fascinated by other students' art, whether it comes from a school across town or from the other side of the world. Because it is visual, art soars over cultural and language barriers. Because it is portable, it can be shipped to other countries with relative ease and low expense.

Exchanges of art require planning, cooperation, and coordination. Art teachers first may wish to exchange art with other schools in their own communities in order to determine the logistic strategies, costs, and time schedules. Once they have established clear procedures with their counterparts in other schools, they can begin to reach further afield and begin turning over some of the correspondence and coordination to responsible students. Students especially enjoy writing to people in other communities, states, and countries. The Internet makes communication easy and almost instantaneous.

The Internet also allows students to develop a dialogue with children in other countries before, during, and after they exchange their art. Johnson and Rauch (2003, n.p.) encouraged children in the southwestern United States to correspond with children in Australia. They discussed their art and lives over the Internet, interspersing electronically transmitted pictures with actual works of art sent by regular mail. Images led to imagery and a search for meaning and understanding on both sides of the Pacific.

Robert Wilson (2005), who teaches at Floral Street Elementary School, in Shrewsbury, Massachusetts, has his students create abstract paintings and prints that serve as backgrounds to inspire other children who paint over them. However, the other children are in another country. Wilson sends his students' background paintings to elementary schools in Japan, South Korea, and India, where children complete the paintings with their own imagery. Wilson was able to make contact with the foreign schools through parents of foreign origin living in his own Massachusetts community.

Mary Frank Sheesley's students regularly exchange art with children in many different countries around the world. They exhibit each other's work and correspond in the Global Art Exchange program. For more about this program, see Case 6.7 in Part II.

Partnerships with Museums

Many museums have lending programs that allow schools to borrow works. Usually the school must assure the lender that the work will be housed in a secure place, such as a gallery that can be locked. A rider on the school's insurance may also be required, but this is largely a formality. Art may also be borrowed from local artists and collectors, who are often delighted to share their art with children and may want to speak at a subsequent opening. Many communities have collectors who have studied their specialty in great depth. Whether their collections are of paintings or porcelain, books, or banjos, students will be intrigued by how much care, craft, and connoisseurship go into cherishing objects.

Borrowed collections add another dimension to exhibiting art. The students will not be as familiar with the works as they are with their own art. They must investigate, inquire about, and interpret them more deeply and in different ways. Their themes and installations become focused in some respects and liberated in others.

Viki Thompson Wylder and Linda K. Johnson collaborated with their students, who selected works from the collection of the Florida State University Museum and curated a well-received show. Case 6.8 in Part II tells more about their adventures.

The Community

There are innumerable venues for exhibiting student art outside school. In the community, banks, stores, malls, offices, public and government buildings, hospitals, and places of worship offer attractive places and interesting opportunities for exhibiting student art. Parents who work in these places can often provide contacts, if not make the necessary decisions themselves. Public places outside the school are generally receptive to exhibitions of student art. People in the community are interested in such art and appreciate its motifs and styles. As noted earlier in the chapter, when exhibiting outside the school, parental permission is usually needed but easy to obtain.

For 20 years, Ralph Westgarth has mounted shows of student work at the Hotel Dieu Hospital in Kingston, Ontario, Canada. See Case 6.9 in Part II for more about this ambitious project.

The Internet

The Internet provides an especially rich venue for exhibiting student art. Many schools now have their own Web sites, and electronic galleries are housed in many of them. Each class may have its own home page, and it is literally possible for every child to display his or her work for the entire world to see.

However, students' privacy must be rigorously protected. Students are easily flattered when it comes to their art. Given this fact, their names, photographs, or other means of identification should never be used in unsecured virtual galleries and digital portfolios, and they should understand the reasons for protecting their privacy. Make such points emphatically to students so they will not try to get around it. Above all, outsiders should not be able to contact students via the school Web site, and students should be warned about chatting with strangers on their home computers, even about their artwork.

Artsonia has a Web site that displays children's art from more than 3,000 schools.

> Most school websites are programmed to display a few pieces of artwork in one or two pages, whereas, on Artsonia, you can display hundreds of pieces of artwork with little or no additional effort. On Artsonia, your students' work is displayed side by side with the work of students their own age from thousands of schools in 100 countries. This enables you, your students and your visitors to see your students' work in the context of the creative work by a global community of students. (Artsonia, 2004)

Artsonia does not allow photographs with identifiable human subjects, especially children, on their Web site. Each student is given a unique screen name and Web address for added privacy and security. Teachers submit their students' work online, or Artsonia will scan them for you. There are lesson plans related to some of the displayed art. Artsonia can be accessed at www.artsonia.com.

Ann Cappetta, who teaches at North Haven High School, in North Haven, Connecticut, maintains an online gallery of student art on her school's Web site. For more about her interesting electronic showcase, see Case 6.10 in Part II.

CONCLUSION

Although staging an art exhibition is a fairly straightforward process, there are endless variations and nuances. Teachers need to supervise students closely, so they may stay on schedule and defuse minor difficulties before they grow into major problems. In the beginning, art exhibitions usually start as modest efforts that are in keeping with the students' and the teacher's abilities. Fortunately, success breeds success, and everyone quickly discovers many other possibilities. The scope and scale of exhibitions can evolve rapidly.

With new possibilities come new alternatives. Trying out different types of themes or installation designs is exciting. Extending the scope of shows into other venues, developing publicity, and opening events add fascinating new dimensions to exhibiting.

As exhibitions become more elaborate affairs, teachers need to keep good records to ensure that all students have several opportunities to exhibit during the school year, as well as take different roles in the exhibition process.

Exhibiting student art provides one of the best ways to advocate for the art program in your school. Exhibition makes the visual arts truly visible. It helps parents and guardians, teachers, and school administrators recognize the beauty and value of art, and it cultivates their support.

Part II

A Gallery of Cases

Theme Development

CASE 1.1: ART EXHIBITION WITH A DESCRIPTIVE THEME

The Ross School is a small private school located in a fishing village in East Hampton, New York. East Hampton boasts a prominent artists' community; many nationally known artists have their homes and studios there. Students in the 5th through 12th grade attend the Ross School. While virtually all its graduates seek higher education, 60% are the first generation in their families to do so (Cross, personal conversation, 2005).

Jennifer Cross (Cross & Pickett, 2002) and Nichelle Wilson-Pickett, her fellow art teacher, work with their students to organize several art exhibitions throughout the school year. The seventh-grade students spend an entire semester orchestrating their major exhibition. Each year they curate a thematic show using the work of artists in the community.

Cross selects the theme of the exhibition and contacts local professional artists who agree to lend their work to the show. Because East Hampton has a long history as an artists' colony, Cross, Wilson-Pickett, and their students are able to draw upon an outstanding array of talent (Cross & Pickett, 2002). For their exhibition *Portraits*, nationally renowned artists who live in East Hampton, such as Chuck Close, Michi Itami, Robert Girard, Linda K. Alpern, Steve Miller, Morgan Monceaux, and Joan Semmel, contributed artwork (Cross, 2000).

Cross and her students visited the various artists' studios, interviewed them, and selected works for the show. They photographed the artists with their work and created their own art using the "big ideas" (Walker, 2001) and techniques of their selected artists. They wrote biographies of the artists and created publicity, labels, and descriptive text to enhance their show. The final exhibition, which the students designed and installed in a large reception area in the Ross School's main building, included examples of their own artwork alongside those of the professional artists. The students also produced an impressive full-color catalog.

The benefits of being involved in a project like this are many for the students. It is a wonderful example of authentic assessment, as the students are actually creating their own bit of art history for their community by documenting the show. They learn to be published writers, designers, photographers, art historians and gallery directors. They also learn to collaborate in a meaningful way. The contacts they make with artists resonate and this, in turn, creates good will and communication between the school and the community at large. At the close of the project, we asked students to write reflections about what they did and what they learned. Students have reported the "Curating an Exhibition" project is one of their most memorable activities. (Cross, 2002, n.p.)

CASE 1.2: ART EXHIBITION WITH A NARRATIVE THEME

From the prehistoric past to the present day, art has told stories. Exhibitions also tell stories wonderfully well. At the Art Institute of Chicago, curators worked with a group of 12 elementary students, dubbed the Art Team, to mount an elaborate exhibition based on art drawn from the institute's vast collection. The museum education staff and curators selected six works that had proved popular with children in the past and that represented different cultures, eras, and ways of telling a story (Sousa, 1997).

> The Art Team was brought into the process at the design development stage, [and] discussed and commented on the concept and selection. Working with the Art Team was more about process than product. . . . They were an advisory team. They had ideas and we worked very hard to get those ideas into the exhibition. (Sousa, personal correspondence, 2004)

The Art Team knew what appealed to them most and how other children would likely approach the selections. They knew what they wanted to know about the works and created unique ways to investigate them. The result was *Telling Images: Stories in Art* (Sousa, 1997).

Each work of art was chosen to tell a story, but in different ways. Bernardo Martorell's *Saint George and the Dragon* is a didactic religious work, intended to convey a familiar story to a devout 13th-century congregation. John Quidor's painting *Rip Van Winkle* represents a traditional narrative scene, illustrating a crucial moment from Washington Irving's popular tale. A seven-foot-tall carved elephant tusk recounts the genealogy of Benin royalty in Nigeria, West Africa. A bronze statue of Vishnu from India conjures up ideas of transformation and good versus evil, while alluding to the many avatars (or human forms) Vishnu may take. Walter Ellison's painting *Train Station* recalls a more recent event, an epic journey north made by thousands of American Blacks during the Great Migration of the 1920s and 1930s (Sousa, 1997).

The children discussed the stories each of these works told, and the museum's curators and architect helped them to realize their vision. *Saint George and the Dragon* was shown as it might have originally appeared, in a context offering additional didactic panels that elaborated on the legend of Saint George. Text described the details of the legend (Sousa, 1997).

As part of the process, the children contemplated Rip Van Winkle's story. They imagined what it would be like to fall asleep and wake up 20 years later. What might have occurred in the interim? The wall across from the painting received a floor-to-ceiling mural of the Catskill Mountains, where the story allegedly took place, in order to create an environment suited to the story (Sousa, 1997).

The imagery of the Benin royal-altar tusk is complex and cryptic. A simplified line diagram of the tusk and an interactive game were developed to help visitors identify the symbolic images found in it. Viewers could press a button to hear one of five recorded stories related to the carved tusk (Sousa, 1997).

Walter Ellison's *Train Station* is a small painting that alludes to his own boyhood migration from the rural South to the industrial North. Several of the children were quite aware of the racial overtones depicted in the work. Sara, a 12-year-old, wrote about the painting:

> My interpretation of the Walter Ellison painting *Train Station* is that the artist is viewing this train station as a young black man. When I have been in a train station, it is not segregated into white/black sections—everyone is together, whether they are in the washrooms, on the trains, or in the actual train station. The most important part, I think, is the signs above the trains. The blacks going north and the whites are going south. I don't think segregation is right. I mean, come on, separating people because of their color just isn't right! I think the painting is good and the painter is in touch with his feelings! (Sousa, 1997, p. 41)

Two of the children on the exhibition team were Hindu, with a rich heritage of Hindu customs, dances, and imagery. They were able to make perceptive suggestions about the statue of Vishnu. During ceremonies, Vishnu is often surrounded by flowers, and so the ceiling of the alcove in which the statue stood was crowned with plastic flowers strung on wires. On the walls, colorful depictions of Vishnu's many avatars were drawn, accompanied by explanatory text and recorded descriptions (Sousa, 1997).

The Art Team met weekly over a 6-month period to discuss and plan the exhibition. A professional architect drafted an installation design and revised it based on the children's critiques of it. The Art Team also worked on the interactive components for each of the installations. In addition, visitors were invited to enter an Interactive Room where they could play and create after being inspired by the exhibition.

CASE 1.3: STUDENT ART EXHIBITION
WITH A METAPHORICAL THEME

Icons + Altars is an annual show of children's art held at the New Art Center in Newtonville, Massachusetts. *Icons + Altars* metaphorically interprets an *icon* as a "picture or image to honor a special person, place or thing;" an *altar* is a "place or structure to honor a person, place or thing." Each year the title reveals a special focus, such as in *Nature Revered* (emphasizing the fall and winter, during which the show takes place), *Origins: Images and Myths of Creation, Sacred Places and Guardian Faces*, and *Young Artists' Visions*.

Ruth Slotnick, who was the New Art Center's education director, says the center's education program spends a lot of time on the creative process. The archetypal themes inspired by *Icons + Altars* resonate deeply with children and can be interpreted in many ways through a variety of media. The children develop metaphors and visual similes, brainstorm, and create specific works for the show based on their deliberations. Ultimately, they address three fundamental questions: "Why do artists make art?" "Where do artists find inspiration to make art?" and "Why is art important to me?" Later, they prepare their works for exhibition.

The wall text from *Sacred Places and Guardian Faces* reads,

> In preparation for the exhibition, our young artists learned how artists around the world interpret their beliefs and transform them into an icon or an altar. In the classes held at the center, they focused on guardian figures as fantasy creatures that protect and bring good fortune to a person or place. Students in ceramics created masks that depict guardian faces. Visual arts 2-D students made collages of guardian figures, while Visual arts 3-D students constructed guardian figures. Other students focused on sacred places, defined as "real or imagined places of personal or cultural importance." Visual arts 3-D students made relief sculptures of sacred places, while painting students developed diptychs and triptychs. (Slotnick, personal correspondence, 2003; see Figure C1.3.1.)

CASE 1.4: STUDENT ART EXHIBITION
WITH AN EMOTIVE THEME

Gauguin asked, "Where do we come from? Where are we? Where are we going?" Our origins conjure up evocative mysteries to be explored, particularly when we are young. "Origins" was the theme of an exhibition curated by students from Wichita High School East and held at the Wichita Center for the Arts, in Wichita, Kansas (Jones, 1993). The exhibition brochure reads:

Figure C1.3.1. *Icons + Altars: Sacred Places and Guardian Faces,* New Art Center, Newtonville.

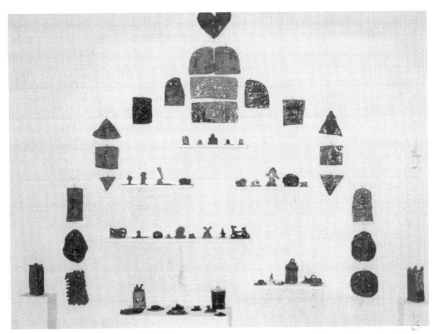

Photo: New Art Center

For us, the students who have contributed time and work toward this exhibit, we are not too far from our origins. As high school students, we are just now beginning to find our place in society, and in doing so, are breaking for the first time from our familial beginnings, our origins. As a generation, we are testing our boundaries, we are pushing the edge. As individuals, we are trying to come to terms with personal triumphs and losses. Each day begins a new start, a new origin. (n.p.)

The brochure goes on to explore origins in terms of our common humanity, beliefs, ancestry and ethnicity, and environment. It concludes:

We draw strength from our origins, because our beginnings nurtured us at our most vulnerable state, birth. Our origins are our home, our mother, our first grade teacher, our favorite food. Origins give us roots and within our origins we find ourselves, passing on our ideas to those around us and, eventually, to our children. As teenagers, however, we are only now starting to sift through our beginnings to find something original—ourselves. (Jones, 1993, n.p.)

Brenda Jones (1993), who teaches at Wichita High School East, observes:

Working in tandem with an art institution [the Wichita Center for the Arts], like a museum or gallery, allows the art student the opportunity to gain an understanding of the philosophy of art as he or she must analyze how various members of the public view art. Further, in planning an exhibit, the student must make practical evaluations of art works. . . . This exhibit is the visual culmination of a long-term examination of the various roles of the art world. Students selected the theme, studied the purpose of a gallery, established a budget, planned for publicity, critiqued and installed works. As a teacher, I have had the unique opportunity to see a tremendous growth in the students as they have examined issues related to the arts and the public. The works on the gallery walls are indeed from students who are still learning, but these works reflect genuine thought and analysis of beginnings, of backgrounds, of all of our origins (n.p.).

CASE 1.5: STUDENT ART EXHIBITION WITH AN HONORIFIC THEME

Each year all the students in Jenn Eisenheim and April Rao's (2001) fifth-grade classes in Concord, Massachusetts, hold a collective retrospective. Every child has a specific area in which to arrange his or her own work. The unique feature of the young artists' selection of artwork in their retrospective is that they began collecting it in kindergarten. When children first enter the school as 6-year-olds, Eisenheim and Rao give the childrens' parents an orientation about the importance of valuing and saving their children's art. Storing every child's art portfolio at school would be impossible, so they encourage the parents to save representative pieces in a portfolio at home. (The parent-teacher-organization even sells portfolio boxes to the parents.) They ask the parents to label and date each work and note any comments their child makes about it. The parents select work with their child, and the work accumulates over the years. Then, in fifth grade, the children go through their portfolios and select a cross section that shows their artistic and creative development over the preceding 6 years. The students arrange their own work in their particular space in the retrospective show. Because each space is limited in size, their choices must be selective as well as representative.

Eisenheim and Rao (2001) ask each student to address five key questions:

- How have I grown as an artist?
- What have I enjoyed about art?
- How can I explain to an audience how I created this work of art and what it means?

- How can I explain to an audience what one of my works *means to me*?
- How do two pieces of my work show how I have grown? (n.p.)

This last question requires the students to compare various works of art.

Finally, the students' statements are edited, composed, and displayed along with their art in the exhibition. Imagine the anticipation and impact these annual retrospective shows have in a small community!

CASE 1.6: STUDENT ART EXHIBITION WITH AN ISSUE-ORIENTED THEME

In 1996, disturbed by the war in Boznia-Herzegovia, Autumn Sears, a preservice art teacher at Virginia Commonwealth University, wanted students in her teaching practicum to become more aware of that tragic conflict. Sears browsed the Internet to find any art being produced in Sarajevo, the capital city in Bosnia. Her search revealed Trio Sarajevo, a small design firm that produces newspapers, magazines, and commercial designs. Trio Sarajevo is known throughout Europe for appropriating familiar logos, such as those of Coca-Cola and Campbell's soup, and altering their slogans with new phrases that call attention to Sarajevo's plight (Green, 1996, p. B3).

Sears downloaded examples of Trio Sarajevo's posters and presented them, along with photographs of the devastation of Sarajevo, to her practicum students in Pam Cosby-Smith's advanced art class at Henrico High School in Richmond, Virginia. They caught on immediately. "The amazing thing is that [Trio Sarajevo are] familiar with American images and themes [through advertising]. It wouldn't work the other way around." Terrance J., an 18-year-old student, reworked the familiar Burger King slogan into a dramatic poster labeled "Sarajevo—Save It Your Way!" "Burger King is my favorite restaurant," [Terrance] explained. "When we were thinking about commercials, their slogan fit right in. It was easy" (Green, 1996, p. B3).

Calandra C. employed the Pepsi wave and added her own slogan, "Sarajevo—The Choice of a New Generation." She said, "Ms. Sears told us about the war there. I thought the young people would like to have their country back, would want to move forward. And the red, white and blue means freedom here in contrast to the war and destruction and terrible things going on there" (Green, 1996, p. B3).

Sears, Mrs. Cosby-Smith, and their students discussed sharing their social concerns with the public by helping their Students organize an exhibition of their posters (see Figure C1.6.1).

We talked about a curator's job and what you have to do to get a show open. Other classes will be coming through to see the show. The students worked

Figure C1.6.1. *Trio Sarajevo*, Henrico High School, Richmond, Virginia.

Photo: Autumn Sears Fesperman

out a schedule and decided who would be docents. "It's a great experience," Cosby-Smith added. "They realized they don't always agree. There have been many discussions about who was going to do what. They're developing mental skills" (Green, 1996, p. B3).

CASE 1.7: THIRD GRADERS SELECTING ART FOR AN EXHIBITION

Michele Dangelo (personal correspondence, 2003), a community volunteer at the Cape Museum of Fine Arts (CMFA), in Dennis, Massachusetts, proposed that the Orleans Elementary School third-grade students (including those with special needs) curate a show from the museum's collection of art. The exhibition would hang in the Marion Crane Gallery, located in the Snow Library Gallery in Orleans, during the month of March, which is Youth Art Month. Everyone was interested, and the Friends of Snow Library offered a grant toward the cost of field-trip buses and other expenses. The first show was held in 1996, and the annual event has continued to the present.

Dangelo and the CMFA director preselected 60 works of art, based on the school theme of the year, for the children to choose from. The works were photographed, information about them was assembled, and the images were mounted on cards and laminated. The art teacher, the school librarian, and the third-grade teachers discussed each selection with the children before their trip to the museum in January. Shortly before the field trip, Dangelo visited the classrooms with actual artworks from the museum, talked with the third graders, and answered their questions. The children were well prepared for her visit to them and for their visit to the museum. Their teachers, the librarian, and the art teacher worked together on a multidisciplinary art curriculum for the exhibition, and they also made a previsit to the CMFA to meet with the director and discuss the project.

In late January, the children made a morning field trip to the CMFA to select the artwork for the show. They also toured the museum, visited the art-storage area, saw an artist at work, had a snack, and viewed a film. The number of parents who volunteered to accompany the children was astonishing—for several, it was their first visit to the museum. All the previously selected work, which the children had viewed in photographs, was displayed for them. Each child had six votes, and each class voted one at a time. Many of the children had already selected their favorite piece, but many changed their minds when they saw the originals. After voting and completion of the other activities, the museum director announced the 30 winners—with a few ties that were broken on the spot. This generated a lot of enthusiasm!

Upon returning to the school, each piece was assigned to two children and the work became part of their curriculum for the following few weeks. The children discussed each piece thoroughly, and after completing their remarks, the information was printed and mounted and finally hung next to the appropriate artwork when it was installed at the Snow Library.

The art teacher developed an invitation, which was sent to all the parents and town officials for the opening reception, attended by many. Artists whose work was displayed were also invited and some made an appearance. During the month of March, the third graders visited the gallery with their teacher, as did students from other grades. Dangelo heard from the art teacher that the children who participated in the 1996 show were more interested in art throughout the elementary school education than those she had previously taught. She felt that the project had long-term, positive effects. After several years as a voluntary coordinator for this event, Dangelo trained her successor.

CASES 2

Exhibition Design

CASE 2.1: STUDENT ART EXHIBITION
WITH A SALON-STYLE DESIGN

M ost art teachers exhibit their students' artwork in annual school or district shows. In many instances, every student is represented by at least one work of art, resulting in a salon style display. Salon exhibitions have a long history dating back hundreds of years. They maximize the number of artworks that can be shown but require good planning and clear themes to avoid a cluttered look. Vikki Chenette, who taught in the Natrona County School District in Casper, Wyoming, developed a popular month-long exhibit with a well-attended reception. Chenette recounts:

Ten elementary art teachers selected themes 3 to 6 months in advance. Each year a geographical area (such as Eastern Europe and Russia), plus four or five broad themes (such as Fantasy Art, the Olympics, Gardens, Animals, or subjects based on art history) were selected. The themes were broad enough that art lessons might produce work related to them. In this way, separate school and grade level artwork were totally mixed up in the [thematic] display areas (personal correspondence, 2002).

Because kindergarten through sixth grade were exhibited, some teachers involved students more than others. Students labeled their artwork after selecting their favorite 2-D and 3-D pieces. For me, even kindergarten students selected what they considered their best work. I involved older students [in Grades 3 through 6] in matting their 2-D work while younger students selected colors for their mats. We developed an opening with students giving arts and crafts demonstrations or teaching techniques. Many students became more motivated after participation in the annual show (personal correspondence, 2002).

CASE 2.2: ART EXHIBITION WITH A LINEAR
INSTALLATION DESIGN

Sherrie Sikora and her students annually mount six exhibitions of art by students, local artists, and local collections in the art gallery at Lincoln Middle School in La Crosse, Wisconsin. The gallery occupies a long, narrow room, measuring 24 feet long by 8 feet wide, that lends itself to linear installations. A glass showcase adjacent to the door provides an inviting overture to the gallery as well as a place for three-dimensional work. As visitors move through the room, they contemplate each work separately and in succession. Rather than the gallery being crowded with many works, the arrangement of a few selected works by four or five students helps viewers savor each one in turn.

Sikora points out,

> Students have the opportunity to experience hanging exhibits, mailing gallery information, using computer skills for graphic work, giving tours of the work displayed, and working with professional artists. This gives them a sense of ownership and optimism important to the overall attitude of the school environment. (personal correspondence, 2002)

CASE 2.3: ART EXHIBITION WITH A SEQUENTIAL
INSTALLATION DESIGN

The seventh-grade students at the Ross School in East Hampton, New York, based the theme of their exhibition, *Drawn from Nature*, on nature and included collections of natural objects with their own art and the art of six professional artists. Lindsey R., a student, writes in the *Drawn from Nature* catalog, "We were assigned jobs, which included writing artist biographies, designing the catalog, taking photographs, interviewing the artists and selecting work. Everybody also participated in installing work into the gallery and giving tours of the final show" (Cross, 2002, n.p.).

Lindsey R. continues:

> This project was integrated with science, art, cultural history and English class. . . . We made our own collections of leaves, insects, and shells. In the exhibit, we made our own little natural history museum to look at like the [ancient] ones in Alexandria, [Egypt]. In English class, we learned about interviewing and editing skills to create artist bibliographies and other text for the exhibit. In our art class we learned about Hellenistic sculpture and how this type of sculpture

shows people realistically. We drew each other's poses and gestures but also had a model come in to draw. When visiting [professional artist] Lauren Jarrett's studio, we had a chance to draw botanical drawings of fresh flowers. We drew from nature when we observed birds in class and at the Morton wildlife sanctuary (Cross, 2002, n.p.).

To help us curate the museum, Lisa Grossman came in from the American Museum of Natural History in New York City. She is an exhibition designer who gave us advice about our exhibit. She told us how we should arrange our things and gave us time to come up with creative ideas for our exhibit, like including sound (we played the CD *Songbirds of Spring* during our exhibition.) To finish up the exhibit we installed the artwork, arranged the catalog, created publicity and prepared a mini-museum education program (Cross, 2002, n.p.).

CASE 2.4: STUDENT ART EXHIBITION WITH A COMPARATIVE INSTALLATION DESIGN

When works of art are paired, their similarities and differences often stand out. Viewers can compare features of each work that might not otherwise be obvious. Peg Koetsch and her colleagues found their students were able to bring a heightened awareness to their exhibition about slavery by contrasting it with the privileged life of plantation owners.

School museums, like their professional counterparts, juxtapose artifacts and experiences to build connections and explain concepts. [At Bailey's Elementary School of the Arts and Sciences in Falls Church, Virginia, fourth-grade] students constructed sequential displays to communicate a coherent body of knowledge. Although individual students or small groups may have immersed themselves in researching a particular issue or question, they had to connect their ideas with those of their peers during the exhibit installation process to tell a multifaceted story that visitors will understand (Koetsch, D'Acquisto, Kurin, Juffer, & Goldberg, 2002, p. 76).

After conducting research at Sully Plantation, a local "living history" museum, several interest groups at Bailey's Elementary chose to illustrate different characteristics of a slave's daily life on a plantation during Virginia's colonial period. The architecture group painted a mural depicting a slave's quarters. The recreation group collected musical instruments resembling those played in Africa. The agricultural group made models of foods produced on the plantation of the period. Not until they brought these components together did students realize that their display did not convey the message of inequality that the students had intended. Finally they resolved to broaden their original concept to compare basic needs as seen through the eyes of a slave and those of a slave owner. After checking their references, students painted a second mural, this one of inside a plantation house, and displayed both murals next to each other (Koetsch et al., 2002, p. 77).

In this project, Koetsch emphasized how visitors learned from the exhibition rather than how the exhibition looked. She asked students, "What is the message you want visitors to learn as a result of going through your exhibit?" Reporting on her use of this technique, she explained, "Once that goal is established, the students decide how to engage visitors in the learning process, which then determines where artifacts will be placed, and usually [leads to] the creation of a hands-on learning center" (personal correspondence, 2002).

CASE 2.5: ART EXHIBITION WITH A SYNOPTIC INSTALLATION DESIGN

Margaret Wood's advanced art students at L. C. Bird High School in Chesterfield, Virginia, began their exhibition project with a trip to the Virginia Museum of Fine Arts, where they met various museum staff, including a curator, a lighting director, an installation designer, a publicist, and a museum educator. The installation designer and publicist described how they begin conceptualizing each exhibition [at the museum] by picking an icon, a dramatic image that embodies the theme of the show and that can be used in the show's publicity and signage. Ms. Wood and her students were able to borrow a dozen photographs from the museum to inaugurate their new art gallery at L. C. Bird High School. The photographs, by such luminaries as Jacob Riis and Lewis Hine, depicted American children between 1880 and 1920, working in factories and farms and trapped in tenements, as well as living in luxurious splendor. The students chose as their icon Hine's poignant image of a young girl toiling in a cotton mill. It became a motif that related all the elements of the exhibition together well (Wood, personal correspondence, 2000).

The Sanders Gallery, named for a revered art teacher who had recently retired, was a former teachers lounge adjacent to the cafeteria. The students painted the room, installed panel doors, and created signage for the show. They borrowed antique farm implements, furniture, books, and toys from teachers and parents to enhance the photographs. Initially, for their installation, they wanted to contrast the squalor of the children in some of the photographs with the affluence of other children. As they researched and discussed the theme in more depth, they found that grouping specific photographs with various antiques seemed to emphasize the content of the photographs more fully. In this way, two starkly contrasting batches evolved into several more complex groupings (Wood, personal correspondence, 2000).

A student who participated in the exhibition process wrote:

> This consistency makes the working of the gallery look and feel more professional. The first part of arranging the work is deciding on a theme that should be illustrated throughout the exhibit and that will have an impact on the viewer, leaving him or her with a certain mood or feeling. [We] spread out all of the photographs, lining them up against the walls. Changes were made based on the subject matter of the images. We began to evaluate and arrange the antiques and artifacts we had acquired. We decided to place the image of two boys in a field above the plow. We then placed a picture of a tap-dancing child behind the radio and near the accordion. Next to the icebox and butter churn, we placed a photograph depicting a kitchen scene. Above the display of toys, we placed images of toys and children at play. Last, we installed a pedestal with a small washboard and a box of soap directly under the image of a little girl washing her doll's clothing. With this arrangement it looks as if the washboard has been taken right out of the photograph (Patrick E., personal correspondence, 2000).

CASE 2.6: ART EXHIBITION WITH A CONTEXTUAL INSTALLATION DESIGN

For 23 years, Robert Sabol (1997) worked with his students in the Children's Art Gallery, in Crawfordsville, Indiana, to produce 39 exhibitions that attracted more than 64,000 visitors. Sabol and his students borrowed artifacts from museums and exchanged art with children in other countries to exhibit in their gallery. Creating an appropriate setting for these cultural items stimulated their ingenuity and ambition.

The educational content of the exhibits was emphasized. Students wrote catalogs and programs to introduce exhibits. Teachers and students visiting the exhibits received these materials and were asked to read them while at the gallery. Videotaped introductions for each exhibition were created and shown to visitors. These videos contained interviews with artists; explanations of media, techniques, and processes; historical and cultural information; and brief presentations of selected works in each exhibition.

The installation of the exhibits was done by the Display Committee. The committee created lists of exhibit topics and themes of interest to them and wrote letters to artists, museums, and organizations requesting materials for exhibits. They also drafted exhibit announcements that were given to classroom teachers and administrators, sent press releases to the local newspaper, and designed school-district publicity campaigns for each exhibit. Sabol describes the exhibition as follows:

> Twenty students, from fourth through sixth grade, were responsible for unpacking, hanging, arranging, labeling, and displaying every exhibition. Many exhibits required construction of special cases or other means of display. Other exhibits were enhanced by creating display environments. One exhibit, for example, had an African village created in the gallery that included junglelike landscaping with freestanding trees, plants, grasses, flowers, and rocks, a full-sized hut made of grass mats, and maps of Africa showing countries where pieces on exhibition were made.
>
> These environments became an important aesthetic element of each exhibit and provided an atmosphere that contributed to the display of the artworks. The Display Committee also created hands-on activities for each exhibit. Because students were not permitted to touch any of the artworks on display, their natural curiosity and interest in touching had to be considered and satisfied elsewhere. A portion of each exhibit thus contained touchable objects. These frequently included musical instruments, books, artists' materials, costumes, jewelry, toys, and other objects related to themes of each exhibit.
>
> As the reputation of the gallery spread, parents, businesses, and people from the community became involved with the program. Openings, receptions, and evening and weekend viewing hours were created to help visitors see the exhibits. Track lighting and electronic security systems were donated, and local businesses supplied materials and space for exhibit publicity. Exhibits came from a variety of sources that reflected children's interests.
>
> The Children's Art Gallery was a successful art education program that allowed students in a small rural community to interact with and experience a wide variety of art forms from a number of historical periods and content. It provided student artists with opportunities to display their works, gain recognition for their achievements, experience producing art exhibits, and care for collected artworks (Sabol, 1997, p. 12).

CASES 3

Exhibition Installation

CASE 3.1: SELECTING AND INSTALLING ART

Laurel G., a student at the Ross School, wrote this preface for the school's brochure *Abstraction Then and Now*, in which she describes the students' curatorial and installation processes: "The whole process of creating this exhibition began with learning about abstract art. In order to do that, Ms. Stotzky, one of our teachers, showed us slides of works by Willem de Kooning, Jackson Pollock, and others, to give us a brief idea of what Abstract Expressionism was" (Cross, 1997, n.p.).

> Before we put the gallery together, we needed to choose the paintings. We visited Arlene Bujese's art gallery where we picked out works of art by Charlotte Park, Robert Motherwell, Carol Hunt, and others. Then we went to Sally Egbert's studio where we chose a few of her paintings. We also picked out a work by Robert Harms. (Cross, 1997, n.p.)
>
> A few days later we started actually designing the installation. Several of the paintings we had chosen had to be eliminated from the list because they didn't fit in with the context of the show, or were too big. These things helped us come to a consensus about what things were to go into the show. We started designing by looking at the room and deciding how much room we had for each painting. Then we decided what paintings looked good together. Once this was done we took the most famous work of art in our show, a print by Robert Motherwell, a first generation Abstract Expressionist, and placed it on the back wall, smack in the middle, with no other works of art around it. Then we took four paintings that looked good together and placed them on the bigger wall. We kept rearranging them until they looked perfect. We hung up the paintings by measuring, and then driving picture hooks into the walls. We had to level them out and make sure that their centers were lined up: we used a level to do that. (Cross, 1997, n.p.)

CASE 3.2: INSTALLING STUDENT ART

Michael Gettings (personal correspondence, 2000), who teaches art at Swift Creek Elementary School, Chesterfield County, Virginia, tells how his students installed their artwork:

> For the big school show I had the fourth- and fifth-grade classes put up the art show. We talked about putting up work for the upcoming Achievement Night and decided that each student would have at least one work on display. For such exhibitions, I collect works starting at the beginning of the year. I try to collect the strongest work. I have the works separated by class and grade level. We discuss the best placement within fire code restrictions. I show them how to tear and roll tape on the back of the work. I divide the class into teams of four or five students. Each team gets a class folder of artwork containing 20 to 30 2-D pieces, a couple rolls of masking tape, and rulers. The rulers are not for measuring but for pressing works against the walls [to prevent fingerprints on artwork and mattes]. I position the team in the hall and show them where they can place the work. I actually draw lines [with chalk] on the walls to show them were they can and cannot place art. It usually takes a 45-minute class period to introduce the lesson and have the team complete one class folder. I circulate around the halls to assist the students and offer guidance.
>
> I only give rough guidelines on the aesthetics of placing the works. I like to see how the students view placing the works. Some groups put them very close together, some in a random fashion, and others practically measure the distances. As the week progresses, they get to see different approaches to the problem, and I'm sure they weigh theirs against the others. It is neat [how the students interact] socially because they really have to work as a team to get the job completed. The students get a lot of positive feedback from teachers and other students who happen to pass in the hall while they are placing the works. In the 4 years I did this at Swift Creek Elementary School, I never had to refer anyone to the office or take disciplinary action. I only had one team that had a problem working together. The students are in charge of taking the works down too. They loved to collect the tape balls! The same approach was used and each team would be in charge of removing a section of work and bringing them back to the art room. The teams usually finished before the 45-minute period was over. I usually had a "bonus activity" like free drawing for the remaining 10 minutes of class.

CASE 3.3: DEVELOPING AN INTERACTIVE INSTALLATION

In the design-development stage of *Telling Images: Stories in Art*, an exhibition at the Art Institute of Chicago (see Case 1.2), the students of the Art Team discussed and commented on, among other works, Martina Lopez's *Heirs Come to Pass, 3*, of 1991. For her project, Lopez originally wanted to conduct an interview via a computer game; however, the technological hurtles proved too great. Lopez, the museum education staff, and the children devised an alternative that brought the viewer back to the original work of art, which they all agreed was their primary goal (Sousa, 1997).

> Because Martina Lopez's photographs are about creating a family history, we [the curators and the museum education staff] decided to collect photographs from the Art Team, other children, and visitors to the museum. We asked contributors to write a story about their photograph, and these and family stories became part of the installation. (Sousa, 1997, p. 65)

Visitors to the exhibit responded with dozens of photographs and explanatory stories, which were then displayed along with Lopez's digital montage and the original source material upon which it was based. In this way the viewers were active (and interactive) participants in the show.

CASE 3.4: CREATING AMBIENCE

Seventh-grade students at the Ross School in East Hampton, New York, recreated the Villa of Mysteries, from Pompeii, in their school café.

> The students were shown reproductions of fresco portraits which had been found in the excavated site that had been buried [by the eruption of Mt. Vesuvius in Pompeii, Italy, in 79 CE]. Many of the original frescos came from one villa called the Villa of Mysteries. These frescoes show motifs related to a mystery cult of Dionysus [also known as Bacchus]. Some scholars think that perhaps the original villa was a meeting place for their ecstatic rituals, but no one is really sure. The meaning of these frescoes is highly debated and remains, ultimately, a mystery. For our project, each student selected a Pompeiian fresco. Students then took digitized photos of one another mimicking the poses in the frescoes. Using their computer skills, they merged their own photos with the images from Pompeii, uniting the two with a fresco look. . . . The students used large-format drafting printers to print their merged images.
> Preliminary sketches were made of the school café as a Pompeiian room. These were based on extensive research of reconstructed Pompeiian villas. Faux columns and stone doorways were created from Styrofoam and paint. One day after school, the seventh graders converted the café to the House of Mysteries by painting the walls [Pompeiian red], attaching the faux columns

and installing large-scale printouts of the altered frescoes they had generated on the computer.

[The Ross School café took on an entirely different atmosphere with its new images and colors.] In this integrated project, the most important contributors and beneficiaries were the seventh-grade students themselves. The students personalized their study of Latin: they became a part of the Latin textbook and the life of Pompeii. Every step related to their larger curriculum: the Hellenistic Age and the influence of Greek art and artists on the Roman empire. (Cross, 2000, n.p.)

CASES 4

Exhibition Publicity

CASE 4.1: PLANNING EXHIBITION PUBLICITY

Paul Terrell Jr. (2003) provides his students in Midlothian High School, Midlothian, Virginia, with this outline for their exhibition publicity campaigns:

Identify and locate media sources (first week)
1. Major newspapers, local newspapers, student newspapers, radio, television.
2. All newspapers have a "life-style" or entertainment section appropriate for the [exhibition] announcement and a listing of cultural events. All radio and most TV stations will carry appropriate community-interest or public service announcements.
3. Using the telephone book, contact the various media you wish to use to find out the names, correct mailing addresses, and schedules of people to contact. ALWAYS FOLLOW THEIR DIRECTIONS TO THE LETTER.
4. In general most media outlets want a two- to three-week lead time before the event.
5. Use media sources that either you use or that you think your target audience uses.
6. If an on-air interview is possible, inquire as to the proper procedure and try to set one up. Such research must be done very early [during the first week].

Write news releases and prepare photographs of artwork
1. Use two news release formats. A. An extended format giving a full but concise description of the event, and B. a short format simply listing the event. Most media outlets will want the full news release sent to the appropriate person or department. But [they may] also want the short listing to be sent to a different person or department for a simple listing section, or short public interest announcement.
2. If you send photographs, there is a very good chance that they will be reproduced. Do not expect the pictures back [unless you supply a self-addressed, stamped envelope, along with a written request].
3. News releases should be no longer than about half of a typed page. The listing release should give only the descriptive title, times, dates, and location.

   4. News release format:
       Release date
       Good-through date
       Contact:
       Contact's telephone number [and e-mail address]
       Descriptive title/heading
       Body of the release: who, what, where, why, how
       Exact location with simple directions
       Dates, including reception dates, times, and special events, such as a
         speaker.
       Hours open to the public
       Phone number the public can use for more information
   5. Listing format: Follow the news release format but exclude the body of
      the release.

Send out news releases during the third week
   1. Your target is to get into the Sunday art section of the newspapers prior
      to opening of the show. Give yourself enough lead time.
   2. One week after you send out the releases, when appropriate, give the
      media people to whom you sent the releases a phone call to confirm.

    One week after sending out the press releases, invite [media representatives] to view the show during a special press day one day prior to the reception date.

(n.p.)

CASE 4.2: EXAMPLE OF A STUDENT REVIEW

The word *Review* covers a lot of territory, and reviews can take many forms. They can be an opinion piece written by an art critic that might appear in a publication, a synopsis of a show that introduces a catalog or brochure, or even an interview with the artist. Kristin C., a seventh grader at the Ross School, wrote this synopsis for the catalog of the show, *Pop Art and Its Legacy*:

> The Pop Art Movement was started in the 1960's by artists who took their inspiration from popular culture and low forms of art such as cartoons, newspapers, coke bottles, advertisements, and everyday objects. Some of the most influential Pop artists were Andy Warhol, Roy Lichtenstein, James Rosenquist and Robert Indiana. Andy Warhol made silkscreens and lithographs of well-known personalities like Marilyn Monroe. He also made a painting of a soup can! Roy Litchtenstein worked in a comic book style, painting characters such as Donald Duck and Mickey Mouse and using images like a ten-dollar bill. James Rosenquist was one of the first to make billboard size paintings, in which he made fun of American consumerism. Robert Indiana used the big bold letters and numbers from commercial images, bright colors found in signs and billboards because he felt they had a way of communicating. . . .

There were a lot of mixed feelings about Pop Art when it first was started. Some people thought it was a great side of art and liked all the bright colors. Others felt it took away from the beauty of traditional art and that it was cheating. They felt it shouldn't be considered art. It is still a controversy now whether people think that it should be called art or not. A lot of people have gotten used to it and decided it was part of life and realized it can be art. Other people still hold strong to what they believe art is and just aren't going to change their minds about it. . . .

All of these artists have been influenced by the Pop Art movement, particularly by the work of Roy Lichtenstein. We realized this when we noticed that each of the artists we visited owned an original Lichtenstein print! (Cross, n.d., n.p.)

CASE 4.3: INTERVIEWING AND WRITING AN APOLOGIA

Seventh-grade students at the Ross School were fortunate to interview the professional artists in their exhibition, *Feeling into Form: Sculpture on the East End.* Their teacher, Jennifer Cross, supplied them with a list of sample questions to ask the artists but encouraged them to think of their own questions. Cross's questions are especially interesting to children and adolescents, yet each contains an important aesthetic concept:

- How long have you been making art? Did you make art as a child?
- Did your parents encourage you to be an artist?
- Who were some of your best teachers?
- What art by others has influenced you?
- How do you get your ideas?
- What do you do if you run out of ideas?
- Do you ever get frustrated when making your art? If so, how do you overcome it?
- Do you listen to music when you make art? What kind?
- What do you consider your greatest accomplishment?
- What do you want people to get from your art?
- Do you miss your art when someone buys it?
- How do you define art?
- What advice would you give to young artists? (Cross, 2003, n.p.).

After interviewing artist Elizabeth Strong-Cuevas, seventh graders Taylor S. and Rowenna C. wrote the following for the exhibition catalog:

Ms. Strong-Cuevas does most of her sculptures of faces. In some of her art there are two or more faces. She uses positive and negative space and the contrast between them. Ms. Strong-Cuevas sometimes makes little models of the big public sculptures she is planning to build. The style of Ms. Strong-Cuevas' art reflects the Egyptian and Mayan art she admires. Her favorite part of doing sculpture is using her hands. Ms Strong-Cuevas said that her art always expresses her emotions. She sometimes likes to listen to Beethoven and Billy Holiday when she is working in her studio. She has one sculpture titled "Always Look Twice." While explaining about her piece she stated that it important to look many times. [Her] artist's quote: "Always look twice, three times, or more." (Cross, 2003, n.p.)

While some of the information in their interview might have been gleaned from other sources, talking with Elizabeth Strong-Cuevas allowed the seventh graders to ask questions and follow them up, pursue new directions of thought, and form their own opinions. They reached beyond their own interpretations of Strong-Cuevas and her art to a confident explanation of it.

CASE 4.4: PREPARING AN EXHIBITION CATALOG

Each year, students at the Ross School in East Hampton, New York, undertake a semester-long project to produce a major exhibition of professional artists living in their community. The exhibition includes a beautiful full-color catalog containing thematic essays, interviews and biographies of the artists, images of individual works of art as well as installation views, examples of the students' own artwork, and interdisciplinary information from other subjects. Individual students interview each of the professional artists who are selected for their show, while others photograph them and their work. Several students learn QuarkXpress in order to produce the spiral-bound gallery-quality catalog that can then be shared with the exhibiting artists, patrons, and other members of the school community. Because the exhibition is a semester-long project requiring several field trips and time away from other classes, the students work with their science, history, and language arts teachers on assignments that integrate these subjects into their catalog (Cross, 2000).

In addition to presenting information gathered from the interviews of professional artists represented in the show, students referred to the artists' resumes, Web sites, art reviews and other written materials. For example, the student writing the Chuck Close biography got her information from a film, books, and articles about the artist. For the *Portraits* exhibition, one student had the job of writing the catalog essay entitled "What is a Portrait?", a work that explored the theme of portraiture and synthesized the whole project (Cross, 2000).

CASES 5

Exhibition Events
and Assessment

CASE 5.1: PLANNING AN EXHIBITION
WITH AN OPENING EVENT

Deborah Diffily teaches kindergarten and first grade in Fort Worth, Texas. A kindergarten science unit on rocks led to a field trip to a science museum. "At the museum the children asked questions and drew pictures. Some selected favorite rocks and sketched them. Others drew exhibit techniques for displaying rocks. The children returned to the classroom determined to make their own museum exhibit" (Diffily, 1996, p. 73). Diffily goes on to recount what occurred back at the school:

> As a class we scouted around our school building and discovered a room in the basement that was not being used. After the children wrote letters seeking permission to use the room for an exhibit, they embarked on a flurry of activities. Every day we had class meetings to decide what we needed to accomplish. We maintained several lists, crossing off what we had done and adding new tasks as we thought of them. Some parts of the planning stages were accomplished by a whole class; some were handled by committees of children. (p. 73)
>
> For weeks the children planned and replanned their exhibit. They made floor plans, arranged furniture, and discussed what should be included in each part of the exhibit. Everyone was involved in deciding how the exhibit should be organized. . . . Another committee worked on the brochure for the exhibit. Still another committee wrote labels to identify the rocks that we had in our exhibit. Following the example of a pictorial display the children had seen during their museum trip, they decided to use various media to create pictures of rocks. These pictures were displayed on the walls for visitors to view as they walked down the stairs into the basement exhibit area. (p. 74)
>
> Parents, grandparents, aunts, uncles, and siblings attended the exhibit opening. The kindergarten children played multiple roles as they greeted visitors, passed out exhibit brochures and refreshments, and explained the exhibit. . . . The museum exhibit project was conceived, planned, and implemented by kindergarten children, but the teacher's role in this project was critical. My role throughout the project was to support the children's efforts, to help them

accomplish their plans without taking over, and to incorporate as many content-area skills into the project as could be done naturally (p. 74).

CASE 5.2: ASSESSING STUDENT LEARNING THROUGH ART EXHIBITION

Tammy McGraw taught art at the Franklin County Middle School in Franklin, Virginia. For a number of years she involved her students in successful art exhibitions.

The learning needed to curate student art began early and continued throughout the school year. Ms. McGraw started each year (or in the case of 6th and 7th grade students, each rotation) by discussing art from the standpoint of exhibiting and appreciating art as well as production. Students learn from the onset that the artistic/aesthetic process remains incomplete until they have prepared their work for display and presented it to their peers and the visitors to the school. They display every work of art upon completion. They also understand that even work displayed on the bulletin board in the classroom cannot arbitrarily be pinned to the board but must be thoughtfully placed in relation to all the other works (Burton & McGraw, 2001, p. 30).

In Ms. McGraw's classes, the variety of tasks and teams involves everyone, even though everyone may not exhibit in each show. In this way, they develop extensive experience throughout the year in assessing their own work and are able to use these skills to choose those pieces from each assignment that will best represent the class. In a sense, they evolve, becoming connoisseurs who truly understand their art; they recognize that this is an essential position to hold in the overall process. (p. 30)

Ms. McGraw's efforts throughout the year culminate in an annual art exhibition that draws the attention of the entire community. Her students develop a theme, an exhibition plan and a timetable well in advance, and plan the publicity, secure parental permissions, design the invitations, signage, and program. Media, local government representatives, school officials, parents and community leaders receive special invitations. The local media covers the event and students from the life skills classes prepare food for the opening reception. (p. 30)

Throughout the school year each class chooses works for the annual show at the end of the year. Eighth grade students select approximately 100 works from this overall collection and conceive an appropriate theme and title for the exhibit. As they complete this process, each student writes a brief declaration to clarify the commonality of the work. The best statement, determined by the students, appears on the back cover of the exhibition program and serves to express their collective thoughts about their work. (p. 30)

Working in teams, they prepare each work for exhibition. Students do all this work. Individuals who have demonstrated outstanding craftsmanship usually cut the mats. They mat and frame each work with quality mat board, foam core backings, glass and good-quality aluminum frames that are relatively inexpensive and easily assembled. We could not—would not—skimp on the display for such an important event. Finally, each work is accessioned. (p. 31)

A special moment for Ms. McGraw occurred when the mother of a severely and profoundly mentally disabled child came to the show to see her child's work. She thanked McGraw for including her child in the event though she had not indicated that she wished to buy the work when she returned the permission form. They walked over to the child's work, one of the most powerful paintings in the exhibit. The brilliant color and energy of the piece radiated incredibly. The mother cried when she saw it; she couldn't believe that her child had done it. "It was, in many ways," McGraw recalls, "my best day as a teacher." Needless to say, the mother purchased the painting, much to the dismay of several other visitors. (p. 31)

CASES 6

Teaching Art Exhibition

CASE 6.1: WORKING WITH AN ARTIST

The Park School in Baltimore, Maryland, is a private, urban school where the arts are a high priority. Carolyn Sutton, the director of arts, and Peter Brunn, the exhibitions educator, work together to produce shows featuring the work of professional artists as well as several grades of Park School students (Brunn, 2003).

Brunn identifies professional artists, such as fiber artist Annet Couwenberg, and schedules an exhibit of their work. Students at various grade levels study the artist's concepts, medium, and techniques, in their own art. To complement Couwenberg's show, *Re-addressing Fiber*, K–4 and K–5 did finger knitting, the first grade wove paper, the second grade quilted, the third grade studied fiber-working tools, the fourth grade made paper and paper cranes, and the fifth grade created a felt tapestry. The second through fourth grades all engaged in felting. Their art was exhibited along with Couwenberg's (in the school gallery). Finally, Couwenberg visited the school and gave gallery talks and assemblies for both the lower and upper students, using a PowerPoint presentation. Members of the community attended receptions and openings as they would professional galleries (Brunn, 2003, n.p.).

As Brunn (2003) points out, the Park School exhibitions program, along with its gallery, honors student artistic work, inspires and showcases classroom projects, locates student creative work within a broader cultural context, provides a forum for the Park community to engage in dialogue, brings the highest levels of contemporary art practice to the Park community, nurtures partnerships and affiliations, and advances the Park School in Baltimore's cultural community (n.p.).

The Park School is able to attract first-class professional artists to exhibit there because of its commitment to quality exhibitions, its reputation, and the ambience and security of its gallery facility.

CASE 6.2: LEASING STUDENT ART

Christa Wise (1997), an art teacher in Saugatuck High School, Saugatauk, Michigan, created a program in which students are able to lease their art to local businesses and patrons for a year. Students, with their parents' permission, submit their drawings, paintings, prints, and collages to three jurors who are local artists and gallery owners. The jurors select two or three works from each grade level from kindergarten through high school. Wise has the works professionally matted and framed to enhance their visual appeal and makes them ready to hang. An engraved nameplate with the student's name and grade accompanies each work.

All the work is placed on view at the Saugatuck-Douglas District Library for a month. Wise publicizes the reception heavily, making it a major community event with food and entertainment. Each work is leased for $100; there is no bidding or competitive pricing. All the works are usually leased in the first 2 hours of the reception. Funds raised during one year are used to underwrite the framing and publicity for the following year. As one businessman put it, "You always worry about how to decorate your office. No matter how you do it, someone is not going to like what you choose. With kids' art, everyone notices and everyone smiles." Patrons agree to hang the artwork in public places, such as their businesses and offices. Private donors could have their leased works displayed in the local health center, library, city hall, or another municipal building. The children's art appears throughout the community. At the end of the year, the framed artwork is returned to the original student-artists.

CASE 6.3: EXHIBITING IN SCHOOL HALLWAYS

Rows of lockers stretch down the centers of halls at Hays High School in Buda, Texas, where Sherry Snowden, who teaches art there, designed "locker toppers." They create back-to-back easel-display areas that straddle the rows of lockers. The school district had them built with stained wood to match the custom display cabinets Snowden had previously designed. More than 600 works of art can be exhibited at a time in this hallway gallery (Snowden, personal correspondence, 2000).

Snowden says,

> [The artwork] is constantly changing. We are housed [near] the counseling center so we get a lot of visitors. People are always stopping in my room to tell me how they enjoy the gallery. So far none of the work has been vandalized. This is almost unbelievable but it shows how much the students' works are respected. One

administrator was so impressed that he purchased a professional mat cutter. I train a team of students to be a mat team. We have been adopted by a local framing store that provides us generously with mat scraps. These help a lot in improving the appearance of the work and its presentation. Our administrators are very good about sending us thank you notes and notes of recognition. I always read them to my students and post them by the door. The students really like to receive them. Some people think high school kids don't care for such things but, believe me, they do! (personal correspondence, 2000)

CASE 6.4: EXHIBITING IN A SCHOOL GALLERY

Ralph Caouette (personal correspondence, 2003) and his Art Club schedule 9 to 11 shows each year in which they present student artists, local professional artists, and artists who are school alumni; they also put on solo senior shows and an annual Youth Art Month exhibition. These shows take place in the Bowes Gallery, named for a revered art educator in Wachusett Regional High School, in Holden, Massachusetts. Wachusett High School is a regional high school serving five local communities. It has the only high school gallery in central Massachusetts. Students do the majority of planning and work required in putting their shows together. Contributing artists are often surprised to find a fully insured, professional gallery in a high school. Although narrow (12' by 36'), the gallery has plate glass windows along both its interior and exterior walls that allow passersby to glimpse the art hanging on standing panels that run the length of the gallery.

The Art Club begins the school year with field trips to the art museum at Smith College and art galleries in Northampton, where they discuss the intricacies of exhibiting art with gallery directors. They hold regular meetings to plan shows, publicity, and receptions. Exhibiting artists frequently collaborate with the students to install their work, lending insights about how they see their own art and how they wish others to see it. The students develop briefs for each show to guide them through the exhibition process. Four events a year have receptions, sometimes with music and refreshments. On other occasions, student docents guide special tours of students (Caouette, personal correspondence, 2003).

Caouette notes that the art program has grown from four to eight teachers since the gallery began, and in their new building, the gallery will double its size and be housed in a prime location. They will also have five art niches around the new school building in which curated artifacts from surrounding communities and historical societies will be displayed (personal correspondence, 2003).

CASE 6.5: EXHIBITING AT SCHOOL EVENTS
AND COMMUNITY EVENTS HELD AT SCHOOL

Anne Ezzelle, the art teacher, (personal correspondence, 2003) includes at least one work by every child in the art show for Back-to-School Night at Reams Road Elementary School in Chesterfield County, Virginia. Each year she chooses a broad theme, such as "Art Around the World," that embraces her whole curriculum yet unifies the exhibition. Ezzelle displays a variety of projects from each grade level.

> My goal in the show is to highlight the ideas that art is for all students and all students can create. The response to the shows has been remarkable. For some parents, it is a very positive contact that they have with the school. I have found that the parents of special education students are especially appreciative that their child can participate in a school event [on a level] equal to other children. Many times their artwork is very remarkable and stands on its own merits. It is very exciting to see the happiness and pride on these students' and parents' faces. (Ezzelle, personal correspondence, 2003)

Ezzelle selects artwork throughout the year. She explains:

> After each project is completed, I usually hang a display of the work in the hall. I mark the art with the student's name but also record it in a special set of class rolls to keep track of what works to hang in the [Back-to-School Night] show. When I take the display down I save it to hang again closer to show night. Because of space, bookkeeping, and time constraints I do most of the choosing of the artwork, but I will ask students to volunteer to let me keep a particular project if I wish to display it again. Children sometimes help matte their artwork (personal correspondence, 2003).

CASE 6.6: EXHIBITING THROUGHOUT
THE SCHOOL—GALLERY OWNERS

George Szekely considers each of his students a "gallery owner":

> Each student in my classes owns a gallery. No, these are not special classes for wealthy children. They are simply students responsible for a designated space in the school to develop an ongoing gallery schedule presenting artworks of their own, designed objects they have found, or guest exhibits. These exhibits have taken place in hallways, libraries, and gymnasiums. Each show

has an idea and a theme, an opening, and suitable advertisement. For some classes, the galleries are small-scale, designed to house miniature exhibits that are models for full-scale art. These "shows in a box" allow students to dream freely in different materials and scales, creating complicated, large exhibits that cannot be funded or prepared in a school. Students learn about preparing exhibits, and each show is discussed with other gallery owners and with audiences. Works for each exhibit are tested in many different selections and placement possibilities, from traditional to highly unusual (Szekely, 1988, p. 155).

Our nationally recognized Gallery Owner Program is in its 10th year [as of 2000] of operation, [and] active in 14 states. The program promotes children's original school exhibits, placed in exciting places throughout the building. Art teachers build a master schedule of gallery owners, projects and assist with the development of literature, openings, and promotional activities. Exhibits reflect the gallery owners' ideas as stated in plan books and are not displays of art class assignments. Some shows highlight the owners' favorite objects, while others coordinate theme shows exhibiting items from relatives, friends, or the school community (Szekely, 2001, p. 24).

Unique aspects of the program include:

1. Children's exhibits are treated as artworks, as an important area of their art education.
2. Through the study of home displays, there is a constant commitment to learning about children as display artists. We recognize that children have unique exhibition skills, experiences, and interests that are different than adult display goals and designs.
3. Children are placed in charge of school exhibits. With guidance from the art teacher, gallery owners learn the roles of curators, researchers, exhibition designers, and publicists. With a belief in the importance of independent art learning, gallery owners develop important skills toward becoming independent artists.
4. Schools open new spaces and surfaces for student displays, allowing placements that may not have existed before. The school community accepts that children's displays look noticeably different from adult exhibits. (Szekely, 2001, pp. 24–25)

CASE 6.7: EXHIBITING BETWEEN SCHOOLS—THE GLOBAL ART EXCHANGE

Mary Frank Sheesley teaches at Tommy Smith Elementary School in Panama City, Florida, but her exhibitions are truly worldwide. Sheesley makes personal contacts through her own travels to other countries, through the United States Society for Education Through Art (USSEA) and the International Society for Education Through Art (INSEA), and through immigrants from other countries. She has sent the artwork of her students to 12 countries and received student artwork from more than 20 countries.

The Global Art Exchange program encourages peace among youth from around the world. The mission of the program is to bring an awareness and knowledge of other nations and cultures to our elementary students. This is done by educating elementary students around the world about each other through an exchange of their art. When they exchange their art, a respect and appreciation of the other culture develops. I believe the basis for world peace begins with each of us through personal connections, such as those provided by the Global Art Exchange program.

Since art is the universal language and can be understood by all, there is no need to learn another language to communicate with students from foreign countries. Making personal connections through art helps build bridges of understanding between people and nations. This connection enables young students to gain additional knowledge and an understanding of other cultures by viewing artwork in that culture.

A photo of the student's family, brought in from home, is attached to their artwork. The saying, "A picture is worth a thousand words," is so meaningful when the picture comes from another culture in a foreign land. From the photos students learn how the people from that culture dress, what type of homes they live in, what type of furniture they have in their homes, the special events the family celebrates, what their countryside is like, and where they go on vacations.

Students also gain additional knowledge by doing research on their own. When one of my students learned a piece of his artwork was going to Hungary, he replied, "I didn't even know there was a country by that name!" He was so proud a piece of artwork created by him had been selected to be part of the Global Art Exchange program, he went directly to the library and did some research on his own. The next week when he came to art class, he pointed to Hungary on the globe and explained to his classmates that was where his artwork was going. He proceeded to tell them interesting facts that he had learned about Hungary. (Sheesley, 2003, n.p.)

Sleesley (2003) recommends sending two-dimensional artwork, mounted simply on heavy paper, by mail. It should be unframed and unmatted. Although in the United States mail service is cheaper than shipping, in other countries postage is usually very expensive. Sending art internationally can be a major expense for foreign teachers. However, mail service in other countries is often more dependable and accessible than shipping heavy crates. By sending just the art, messages from the students, and photos and letting the recipient prepare them for exhibition, teachers are more easily able to share their students' art around the world. When teachers here receive unmatted artwork, it provides excellent opportunities for students to perform all the duties carried out by curators and exhibitors, including accession, documentation, and preparation for exhibition.

Notably, Sleesley (2003) does not return the artwork; nor do her students expect to get their artwork back. They understand from the start that when their artwork is selected, the exchange is permanent. This eliminates the need for an expensive return mailing and allows each teacher to add to his or her permanent collection of student art from around the world.

Sheesley gives a certificate to each student whose artwork is exchanged. The certificate notes the student's contribution to understanding among nations and to world peace. For youngsters who may feel that they have little influence on world events, this certificate means a great deal. She points out, "Given the opportunity to view artwork from different countries, students learn to respect and appreciate each others' cultures at a very young age" (Sheesley, 2003, n.p.).

Sheesley (2003) recommends making personal, teacher-to-teacher contacts, without any "middlemen," such as agencies or governments. The Internet greatly facilitates communicating with other teachers and arranging exchanges directly. Sheesley plans an exchange with her counterpart in another country months ahead so both have ample time to prepare students, make and select art, and ready it for mailing. As the due date draws near, she confirms via e-mail that the other teacher is also ready to send his or her package. In this way both teachers receive shipments soon after they have mailed their own.

CASE 6.8: EXHIBITING ART BORROWED FROM MUSEUMS

Viki D. Thompson Wylder, curator of education at the Florida State University Museum of Fine Arts, and Linda K. Johnson, an art instructor from Deerlake Middle School in Tallahassee, teamed up to have eighth-grade students curate an exhibition of art selected from the Florida State University Museum's collection. Wylder and Johnson (2002) planned the project well in advance, including field trips to the museum, learning about museum procedures for handling and accessioning artworks, and selecting and researching works.

The students selected a variety of works from the museum's collection; among them were African sculpture, contemporary painting, Native American baskets, glassware, prints, Oriental porcelain, and pre-Columbian ceramics. By working out a theme after they selected the art objects, the students realized that "deciding what our theme would be was the hardest part. No one wanted to omit the wonderful objects that they came to know while exploring the collection, yet how could we get them all to relate to each other[?]" (Wylder & Johnson, 2002, n.p.). Finally, they devised an equally broad theme, "Masterful Works from Diverse Lands," to encompass the full range of their selections. They drew a scaled blueprint to decide where each work of art could be placed to its best advantage. The students also learned about accessioning art and preparing didactic labels for each work, as well as writing publicity for the show. Finally, with the help of the museum staff, they participated in installing the exhibition.

Marnie E., a student, wrote:

> My friend, Angelina McC., and I are researching and putting together the African art section. We have some really neat artifacts and doing the research is challenging yet fun. Our teacher, Ms. Johnson, is encouraging us to go outside the box to do research. Not only have we used the internet and books, but we have done phone and personal interviews, visited other libraries and visited places with information about our area. (Wylder & Johnson, 2002, n.p.)

CASE 6.9: EXHIBITING IN THE COMMUNITY

Begun in 1986, the Students' Art Gallery at the Hotel Dieu Hospital in Kingston, Canada, has hosted exhibitions of children's art throughout their facility, from the Child Development Centre, to the Ears, Nose and Throat Department, to Almost Home, a space that functions as home away from home for hospitalized children and their families. More than 160 framed works are included in each show, and a new exhibition is installed every 3 months. Most of the works come from schools in the Eastern Ontario region including Limestone District Schools, Algonquin Lakeshore District Schools, and several independent schools. Ralph Westgarth (1996), a teacher at Elginburg Public School, reports:

> The installation of each new exhibition is celebrated with an official opening to which the artists, their parents, teachers and principals are invited. Certificates are presented to the artists, and all students are photographed with their artworks.
>
> Reaction to the Gallery in the hospital has been enthusiastic. While a recent show was being installed, a youngster who was on his way to an appointment exclaimed: "Wow, dad, look at that!" He took a couple of steps and again yelled, "Wow!" A few more steps, and a third "Wow!"
>
> The generosity of young artists is remarkable, for they have been willing to part with their cherished achievements (often "the best thing I ever drew") for several months. An estimated 15,000 to 20,000 people walk through the Gallery in a year and newspaper coverage for each opening is excellent advocacy for art education.
>
> From the onset, the Students' Art Gallery has pursued five main goals:
>
> 1. to demonstrate that the hospital community recognizes the value of creative activities in the total growth and development of every child.
> 2. to encourage children and teenagers to perceive the hospital as a non-threatening place by familiarizing them with the setting without involving any kind of medical treatment,

3. to reduce the anxiety level of those who visit the Child Development Centre and the Children's Outpatient Centre by enhancing the appearance of the hospital environment,

4. to provide a non-competitive and widely accessible forum for meaningful student art work, and

5. to enable young people to experience the deep sense of satisfaction that comes from helping others to feel better

(p. 7)

CASE 6.10: EXHIBITING ON A WEB SITE

Ann Cappetta (personal correspondence, 2002), Sheri Schwartz, and Christine Oulevy curate a virtual Web Museum for the North Haven, Connecticut, schools that serve the entire school district. Located on the North Haven Public Schools Web site at www.north-haven.k12.ct.us, the Web Museum showcases elementary, middle, and high school art in separate electronic galleries. The medium of each work and the age of the child-artist are listed, but no names are given. Some of the works have hyperlinks to the lesson plans that inspired them. An introductory page outlines the schools' art program and curricular goals of the Web Museum. Other links, such as "Art for Thought," cites written student responses to aesthetic questions, while the Art Calendar lists events art-related events throughout the school district. A Student-Curated Show and The Art Corner "encourages student involvement in the electronic virtual gallery and provides a showcase for [North Haven] students" (Cappetta, personal correspondence, 2002). The Web Museum provides continuous visibility for student art.

APPENDIX

NAEA Policy on Contests and Competitions

Occasionally, exhibiting art is confused with contests and competitions involving art. Many teachers and parents hold well-justified feelings that contests and competitions pit students against one another and are efforts to glorify a few works of art or talented students over many others. That is not the goal of exhibiting student art as described in this book. In *Exhibiting Student Art* I describe methods for presenting art in ways that support student expression and advance a substantive, comprehensive art education. Students require sufficient emotional maturity to separate the concept of losing from the idea of rejection as a person (Davis, 1998). When exhibitions are thoughtfully planned and presented, competition should not be a factor. Incentives, such as prizes and awards, should be avoided.

In March 2001, the National Art Education Association (NAEA) produced its "Policy on Contests and Competitions." It is reproduced below in its entirety.

> The National Art Education Association endorses only supervised and thoughtfully presented art contests and competitions at the elementary, middle, and high school levels. The nature and purposes of contests for students at these levels are often incompatible with several of the tenets of a quality art education advocated by NAEA.
>
> Art experiences need to reflect the national standards of a comprehensive art education. They may reflect any or all of the four components: studio production, art history, aesthetics, and criticism. Too often contests and competition focus only on the final product of an isolated and arbitrary studio experience.
>
> Art education is grounded in age-appropriate developmental practices. Elementary lessons focus on process, exploration, and initial experience with skills and concepts relating to art. Middle school lessons build upon exploration and broadening of skill and concept development. High school art courses integrate the components of a comprehensive art education toward a deeper understanding of art and the refinement of the student's personal expression.

The art teacher must carefully consider and evaluate each contest and competition based upon these criteria:

1. The endeavor is educationally relevant and instructionally valuable.
2. National visual arts standards are supported.
3. Expectations are developmentally appropriate.
4. The contest or competition fits into the instructional sequence without disruption.
5. The structure, procedure, and timeline are reasonable.
6. Particular products or businesses are not endorsed.
7. The purpose and audience are compatible to the goals of art education.
8. Support and recognition are given to all participants without exploitation.
9. Qualified judges select work based on published criteria.
10. Participation is optional for students.
11. Prior parental permission is obtained for release, publication, and reproduction of students' names and artwork

Contests and competitions in art are *desirable* in cases when:

- The nature and purposes are compatible with the standards of a comprehensive art education and the goals and objectives of the school's art education program.
- The topic has educational value and meets the needs, interests, and concerns of the learners and teachers.
- The display of student work demonstrates the instruction, standards, thought processes, and creative problem solving strategies involved in artistic learning.
- Students can participate in the contest or competition in a variety of roles other than making art, including setting up the display or acting as jurors, judges or docents.
- Recognition is given to all children whose work is submitted at the school level as well as those selected for final competition.
- Opportunity is provided for public recognition for the quality work produced by children under the tutelage of a qualified art teacher.
- Art teachers are given the opportunity to provide feedback to the sponsor and positively influence future contest initiatives by community groups. There are alternatives to contests; art teachers need to be vocal and willing to work with the community to find other avenues to support both the needs of the community and the educational interests of their students.
- Qualified art teachers are provided an opportunity by the initiating agency to participate in the planning and development of the contest or competition.

Contests and competitions in art are *undesirable* in cases where:

- One student or one artwork is singled out as being intrinsically superior over another, especially at the elementary level. This is counter to the belief that art education should be directed toward developing the creative potential of a wide spectrum of student capabilities.

- Standardization of skill or technique is specified or encouraged. This practice limits student expression instead of developing diversity of expression.
- Artistic expression is compromised, and students, as well as teachers, are exploited by the interests of the sponsors. This is counter to the belief that effective instruction is based upon the needs, interests, and purposes of learners and teachers along with local, state, and national art curricula and standards.
- Participation and completion requires too much instructional time. Many students, especially at the elementary level, often meet once a week, or less, for art instruction. Diverting this precious instructional time may not be in the best educational interests of the students.

(NAEA, 2001)

In addition, art teachers should apprise their students of ethical parameters related to art submitted for contests or competitions, and refuse any works which raise doubts as to their originality or authenticity.

No work which has been directly copied from any published source should ever be entered into a competition unless the student has creatively modified or reinterpreted the original work using the student's own vision or style. Only work which is the unique creation of the individual student should be entered in competitions. Art teachers must be vigilant in making a distinction about the difference between blatant copying and inventive incorporation of borrowed motifs for a creative statement (NAEA, 1988).

References

Altshuler, B. (1994). *The avant-garde in exhibition: New art in the 20th century.* New York: Abrams.

Artsonia. (2004). www.artsonia.com.

Bass, K., et al. (1997, fall). *The educationally interpretive exhibition: Rethinking the display of student art.* Reston, VA: National Art Education Association.

Belcher, M. (1991). *Exhibitions in museums.* Washington, DC: Smithsonian.

Bingham, D. (1994, fall). *Some guiding principles: Gallery teaching for school students at the J. P. Getty Museum.* [*Advisory NAEA*]. Reston, VA: National Art Education Association.

Brunn, P. (2003, April 4). *Enhancing curriculum across disciplines with an art exhibition program.* Paper presented at the annual meeting of the National Art Education Association, Minneapolis, MN.

Burton, D. (2001). How do we teach? Results of a national survey of instruction in secondary art education. *Studies in Art Education, 42*(2), 131–145.

Burton, D. (2004, April 18). *Exhibiting student art: A survey.* Paper presented at the meeting of the National Art Education Association, Denver, CO.

Burton, D. (2005, Spring). *Show me the money.* [*Advisory NAEA*]. Reston, VA: National Art Education Association.

Burton, D., & McGraw, T. (2001). Students as curators. In B. Zuk & R. Dalton (Eds.), *Student art exhibitions: New ideas and approaches* (pp. 28–32). Reston, VA: National Art Education Association.

Carter, R., DeMao, J., & Wheeler, S. (2000). *Working with type: Exhibition.* Crans-Pres-Celigny, Switzerland: Rotovision.

Cross, J. (1996). *Hidden horizon: An exhibition of Long Island landscapes.* East Hampton, NY: The Ross School.

Cross, J. (1997). *Abstraction then and now.* East Hampton, NY: The Ross School.

Cross, J. (2000). *Portraits: An exhibition catalog.* East Hampton, NY: The Ross School.

Cross, J. (2002). *Drawn from nature.* East Hampton NY: The Ross School.

Cross, J. (2003, April 5). *Students as curators: The sculpture show.* Paper presented at the annual meeting of the National Art Education Association, Minneapolis, MN.

Cross, J. (n.d.). *Pop art pavilion.* East Hampton NY: The Ross School.

Cross, J., & Giardi, D. (2003a), *Feeling into form: Sculpture from the East End.* East Hampton NY: The Ross School.

Cross, J., & Giardi, D. (2003b). *Students as curators: student sculptures.* Paper presented at the annual meeting of the National Art Education Association, Minneapolis, MN.

Cross, J., & Pickett, P. (2002). *Students as curators.* Paper presented at the annual meeting of the National Art Education Association, Miami, FL.

Cross, J., & Wilson-Pickett, P. (2000). *Students as curators.* Paper presented at the annual meeting of the National Art Education Association, Los Angeles, CA.

Czajkowski, C. W., & Sikora, M. (2003, April 6). *Interactives in special exhibitions.* Paper presented at the annual meeting of the National Art Education Association, Minneapolis MN.

Danto, A. (1998, January). American realities. *Art Forum,* 92.

Davis, C. (Ed.). (1998, Spring). *NAEA policy on contests and competitions.* [*Advisory NAEA*]. Reston, VA: National Art Education Association.

Davis, C. (Ed). (2001, March). *NAEA policy on contests and competitions.* [*Advisory NAEA*]. Reston, VA: National Art Education Association.

Diaz, S. B. (1998). *Sin fronteras: Handbook for creating mobile museums in barrio schools.* Madison, WI: Madison Children's Museum.

Diffily, D. (1996, January). The project approach: A museum exhibit created by kindergarteners. *Young Children,* pp. 25–27, 31, 32.

Eisenheim, J., & Roe, A. (2001). *Elementary portfolio retrospectives.* Paper presented at the annual meeting of the National Art Education Association, New York.

Gardner, J., & Heller, C. (1960). *Exhibition and display.* London: Batsford.

Gibson, W. J. J. (1961). *Synectics.* New York: Collier.

Graphik Dimensions Limited. (2005). www.pictureframes.com.

Green, B. (1996, May 10). Art students use ad slogans, logos for "Project Sarajevo." *Richmond Times-Dispatch,* p. B3.

Hampe, D. (2003). *Exhibition as authentic assessment.* Paper presented at the annual meeting of the National Art Education Association, Minneapolis, MN.

Harrington-Macklin, D. (1994). *The team building tool kit.* New York: Amacon, American Management Association.

Irvine, H. (1997, Winter). *Building support for school art programs.* Part II: *In the community.* [*Advisory NAEA*]. Reston, VA: National Art Education Association.

Irvine, H. (1999, winter). *Significant differences between outreach and advocacy.* [*Advisory NAEA*]. Reston, VA: National Art Education Association.

Johnson, M. (2003). *Exhibition design handbook: Course reader 433304845B.* San Francisco: San Francisco State University.

Johnson, M., & Rauch, K. (2003, April 7). Searching for Meaning in Research. Paper presented at the annual meeting of the National Art Education Association, Minneapolis, MN.

Jones, B. (1993). *Origins: an exhibition catalog.* Wichita, KS: Wichita Center for the Arts.

Koetsch, P., D'Acquisto, L., Kurin, A., Juffer, S., & Goldberg, L. (2002, September). Schools into museums. *Educational Leadership,* pp. 74–78.

Luehrmann, M. (2003, spring). *Developing a partnership with the principal.* [*Advisory NAEA*]. Reston, VA: National Art Education Association.

Mack, S. (1999, November). *The purpose of art*. Paper presented at the meeting of the Virginia Art Education Association, Richmond, VA.

Matthias, D. C. J., & Walton, C. (1997, fall). Storytelling in art museums. [*Advisory NAEA*]. Reston, VA: National Art Education Association.

McAlpine, A., & Giangrande, C. (1998). *Collecting and display*. London: Conran Octopus.

McLean, K. (1993). *Planning for people in museum exhibitions*. Washington, DC: Association of Science-Technology Centers.

McQuaid, M. (1996). *Lilly Reich: Designer and architect*. New York: Museum of Modern Art.

Maymont Elementary School. (1998). *Children's art auction*. [Brochure]. Richmond, VA: Author.

Sabol, R. (1997). Art exhibits by children for children: The children's art gallery. *INSEA News*, 3(4), 11–12.

Serrell, B. (1996). *Exhibit labels: An interpretive approach*. Walnut Creek, CA: Altamira.

Sheesley, M. F. (2003, April 4). *Global art exchange*. Paper presented at the annual meeting of the National Art Education Association, Minneapolis MN.

Sousa, J. L. (1997). *Telling images: Stories in art*. Chicago: The Art Institute of Chicago.

Staniszewski, M. A. (1998). *The power of display: A history of exhibition installations at the Museum of Modern Art*. Cambridge, MA: MIT Press.

Szekely, G. (1988). *Encouraging creativity in art lessons*. New York: Teachers College Press.

Szekely, G. (2001). The display art of children. In B. Zuk & R. Dalton (Eds.), *Student art exhibitions: New ideas and approaches*. Reston, VA: National Art Education Association.

Taylor, B. (1992). *CAEA student exhibition handbook*. Los Angeles: California Art Education Association.

Taylor, P. G. (2002, September). Singing for someone else's supper. *Art Education*, 46–52.

Terrell, P., Jr. (2003). *Publicity handout*. Midlothian, VA: Midlothian High School.

Turner, J. (1998). *Designing with light*. Crans-Pres-Celigny, Switzerland: RotoVision.

Wale, I. (1999, March). *Presenting an all-student art exhibit (art fair)*. Paper presented at the annual meeting of the National Art Education Association, Washington, DC.

Walker, S. R. (2001). *Teaching meaning in artmaking*. Worcester, MA: Davis.

Weisman, E., & Hanes, J. M. (1999, Spring). *Developing thematic content for the art classroom*. [*Advisory NAEA*]. Reston, VA: National Art Education Association.

Westgarth, R. (1996, winter). Kingston's students' art gallery. *CSEA Viewpoints*, 7.

Wilson, R. (2005, March) *Collaborative art: A worldly exchange*. Paper presented at the annual meeting of the National Art Education Association, Boston.

Wise, C. (1997, March). *Art à Loan*. Paper presented at the annual meeting of the National Art Education Association, New Orleans, LA.

Wylder, V. D. T., & Johnson, L. (2002, March). *Eighth graders as museum curators*. Paper presented at the annual meeting of the National Art Education Association, Miami, FL.

Index

Accessioning artwork, 47–49, 71, 72, 80

Administration, 5, 64, 76, 86, 93; and benefits of exhibits, 6, 108; and dismantling exhibits, 80; and empty spaces as places for art, 100, 104; and installation, 51, 56; and publicity, 67, 72; and support for exhibits, 97, 99

Advertising, 65, 66–68, 81

Algonquin Lakeshore District Schools (Canada), 144

Alpern, Linda K., 111

Altshuler, B., 29

Ambience, 5, 19–20, 37, 50–51, 61, 63, 75, 77, 85, 121, 125, 128–29, 137

American Museum of Natural History (New York City), 122

Apologia, 69, 70, 71, 72–73, 132–33

Arranging artwork, 47, 55–59

Art clubs, 96–97, 139

Art Institute of Chicago, 17, 60, 112–13, 128

Artists, 29, 60, 93; local/community, 76, 121, 133; professional, 121, 133, 137; in residence, 88; statements by, 70–71; visiting, 76; working with, 88–89, 137

Artsonia, 107

Assessment, 2, 3, 4, 72, 80–84, 85, 111–12, 135–36

Auctions, 98

Audience. *See* Viewers

Avant-garde, 29, 60, 92

Awards/prizes, 89–90, 147

Bailey, Mrs.: exhibition by class of, 13–14, 22–24, 27, 32–33, 40–41, 44–45, 57–58, 65–66, 78–79, 84

Bailey's Elementary School of the Arts and Sciences (Virginia), 37, 122–23

Balance, 34, 37

Barlow, Paige, 87

Barr, Alfred Jr., 30, 34

Bass, K., 35

Beallsville, Maryland, 61

Bearden, Romare, 77

Belcher, M., 27

"Big ideas," 20, 111

Bingham, Diane, 36

Board, school, 67, 72, 93, 104

Borrowing artwork, 96, 102, 106, 111–12, 123, 124, 143–44

Bowes Gallery (Massachusetts), 102, 139

Boznia-Herzegovia, 117–18

Briefs, 3, 11, 39–41, 42, 46, 65, 80, 82, 83, 93

Brochures, 65, 66, 70, 71–72, 97, 114–15, 131

Brunn, Peter, 89, 137

Budget, 12, 97. *See also* Resources

Bujese, Arlene, 126

Burton, D., 1, 95, 97, 135

Caouette, Ralph, 102, 139

Cape Museum of Fine Arts (Massachusetts), 27, 118–19

Cappetta, Ann, 107, 145

Carter, R., 30

Case studies, 4. *See also specific topic or school*

Cataloging, 55

155

Catalogs, 4, 65, 66, 69, 72, 84, 97, 98, 111, 131–32, 133
Cave Creek, Arizona, 104–5
Ceremonies, 58, 61
Checklists, 41–44, 80, 83, 87
Chenette, Vikki, 34, 120
Children's Art Gallery (Indiana), 38, 39, 79, 124–25
Cleanup, 50
Clohessy, Sharon, 49
Close, Chuck, 111, 133
Collaboration, 5, 106, 112
Color, 20, 34, 35, 61, 66–67, 102
Commemorative exhibits, 20–21
Community: artists in, 76, 121, 133; and confrontational art, 93; and empty spaces as places for art, 100, 103, 106; exhibiting student art in, 106, 138, 144–45; and social dynamics of exhibitions, 5; and support for exhibits, 96, 97, 98, 99; and teaching art exhibition, 93, 96, 97, 98, 99, 100, 103, 106
Comparative design, 32–33, 35–37, 45, 46, 122–23
Competitions, 89–90, 138, 147–49
Concord, Massachusetts, 116–17
Confrontational art, 90, 91, 92–94
Consensus building, 6, 12–14
Contextual design, 38–39, 46, 124–25
Controversial artwork, 90–94
Cooperation, 5, 6, 32, 56, 105
Cosby-Smith, Pam, 117–18
Couwenberg, Annet, 137
Criteria, 21–27, 28, 89, 93
Cross, Jennifer, 15, 16, 19, 35, 36, 62, 69–70, 72, 88, 96, 111–12, 121–22, 126, 128–29, 131–33
Curators, 61, 63, 81, 88, 93; and briefs, 39, 40–41; class as, 11; and design, 40–41; and events and assessment, 74, 75, 85; importance of communication by, 31–32; and publicity, 64, 65, 67, 69; role of, 11; teachers as, 11; teams as, 11–14; and themes, 11–14; and timetables and checklists, 41

Curriculum, 81, 84, 86–87, 119
Custodial assistance, 51, 80
Czajkowski, C. W., 59

D'Acquisto, L., 122–23
Dangelo, Michele, 27, 118–19
Danto, Arthur, 13, 33
Davis, C., 147
Deerlake Middle School (Florida), 143–44
Degas, Edgar, 59
DeMao, J., 30
Descriptive themes, 3, 15, 22, 25, 28, 111–12
Design/designers, 29–30, 74; and ambience, 61, 63; and briefs, 39–41; case studies about, 120–25; and checklists, 41–44; function of, 45; and installation, 33–39, 55, 56, 61, 63, 122, 123; legal considerations for, 94; overview about, 45–46; and publicity, 64, 65, 66, 67, 123, 124–25; and scale models, 44–45; as step of exhibition process, 2, 3, 29–46, 86; and themes, 20, 26, 28, 31–32, 33, 34, 38, 46, 120, 123, 124; and timetables, 41–44; and working with artists, 88. See also type of design
Diaz, S. B., 47, 56, 60
Didactic themes, 3, 15–17, 25, 28
Diffily, Deborah, 75, 134–35
Dismantling exhibits, 80, 103, 105, 127
Display panels, 51–52
Districtwide shows, 34, 104–5
Docents, 61, 75–76, 84, 93, 117
Donors, 72, 76, 97, 138
Drayage, 80
Dürer, Albrecht, 13–14, 22, 32, 66

Egbert, Sally, 126
Eisenheim, Jenn, 21, 116–17
Elginburg Public School (Canada), 144–45
Ellison, Walter, 112, 113
Emotive themes, 3, 15, 19–20, 22, 25, 28, 70, 114–16

Empty Bowls project, 99
Empty spaces: as places for art, 99–107
End-of-school-year shows, 34
Episodic design, 38
Events, 3, 31, 88; case studies about, 134–35, 140; in community, 100, 103; and installing the exhibit, 60–61; in schools, 66, 100, 103, 140; as step of exhibition, 2, 4, 74–85. *See also* Openings; Receptions
Exchange of artwork, 95, 105, 124, 141–43
Exhibitions, art: as advocacy for art, 99; basic principles of, 26–27; benefits and functions of, 1–2, 4–5, 6–7, 20, 74, 80–81, 86, 108, 111–12; developing programs of, 87–88; developing support for, 96–99; as educational process, 2; and history of art, 29–30, 45–46; length of time for, 79–80, 104, 105; maintaining the, 79–80; size of, 28, 41, 55; as social events, 93; sources of ideas for, 12–13; vision/goals of, 21. *See also specific topic*
Exposition, 65, 68–72
Ezzelle, Anne, 103, 140

Feedback, 6, 81–82, 97, 127. *See also* Assessment
Festivals, 34, 104
Fire codes, 93, 94, 127
Floral Street Elementary School (Massachusetts), 105
Florida State University Museum of Fine Arts, 106, 143–44
Fort Worth, Texas, 134–35
4-D art, 52–53, 58–59
Franklin County Middle School (Virginia), 81, 135–36
Fund-raising, 97, 138

Galerie Beaux-Arts (France), 29
Galleries, 97–98, 101–2, 106, 139, 140–41
Gardner, James, 74

Gettings, Michael, 50, 58, 94, 127
Giangrande, C., 31, 34
Giardi, Diana, 19
Gibson, W.J.J., 18, 60
Girard, Robert, 111
Global Art Exchange, 105, 141–43
Goldberg, L., 122–23
Goya, Francisco José de, 20
Gragnolati, Marilyn, 6
Graphik Dimensions Limited, 50
Green, Barbara, 117–18
Grossman, Lisa, 122

Hampe, Diana, 71
Hanes, J. M., 13
Hanging artwork, 56–58, 105, 121, 138
Harms, Robert, 126
Harrington-Macklin, D., 13
Hays High School (Texas), 101, 138–39
Heller, C., 74
Henrico High School (Virginia), 116–18
Hilgemann, Carol, 96
Hine, Lewis, 123
Honorific themes, 3, 15, 20–21, 25, 28, 116–17
Hotel Dieu Hospital (Canada), 106, 144–45
Hunt, Carol, 126

Icons, 67, 123
Indiana, Robert, 131
Installation, 12, 26, 31, 88, 107; and ambience, 63; case studies about, 126–29; and confrontational art, 93, 94; and design, 33–39, 55, 56, 61, 63, 122, 123; and empty spaces as places for art, 103, 106; and events and assessment, 74, 81, 84, 85; interactive, 59–60, 63, 70–71, 128; and legal considerations, 94; overview about, 61–63; and publicity, 55, 64, 65, 66, 70–71; as step of exhibition process, 2, 3, 47–63; steps in, 47–59; and theme, 20, 26, 51, 54, 55, 60–61, 62, 63

Insurance, 95–96, 106
Interactive installation, 59–60, 63, 70–71, 128
International Society for Education Through Art (INSEA), 141
Internet, 66, 68, 69, 95, 105, 106–7, 143, 145
Interviews, 65, 68–70, 73, 88, 111, 131, 132–33
Irvine, Hope, 54, 72, 82, 97
Issue-oriented themes, 3, 15, 21, 22, 25, 28, 54, 117–18
Itami, Michi, 111

J. P. Getty Museum (California), 36
Jarrett, Lauren, 122
Johnson, Linda K., 106, 143–44
Johnson, Mark, 67–68, 105
Jones, Brenda, 20, 114–16
Juffer, S., 122–23
Juried shows, 89–90, 138, 147–49

Koetsch, Peg, 37, 122–23
Kruger, Barbara, 60
Kurin, A., 122–23

L. C. Bird High School (Virginia), 38, 123–24
Labels, 54–55, 58, 60, 65, 105, 111
Leasing artwork, 138
Legal considerations, 94–96
Lighting, 30, 52, 53, 61, 102
Limestone District Schools (Canada), 144
Lincoln Middle School (Wisconsin), 34–35, 121
Linear design, 26, 32, 33, 34–35, 46, 121
"Locker toppers," 101, 138–39
Lopez, Martina, 60, 128
Luehrmann, Michael, 96, 99

Mack, Stevie, 18
Magritte, René, 60

Maintaining the exhibit, 79–80
Martin, Rose, 62
Martorell, Bernardo, 112, 113
Matthias, D.C.J., 77
Maymont Elementary School (Virginia), 98
McAlpine, A., 31, 34
McGraw, Tammy, 81, 135–36
McLean, K., 5, 74
McQuaid, M., 30
McTighe, Daisy, 2
Media, 27, 34, 52–53, 58
Meis, Klista, 6
Metaphorical themes, 3, 15, 17–19, 22, 25, 28, 32, 45, 114
Midlothian High School (Virginia), 130–31
Miller, Steve, 111
Mohor, Carole, 6
Monceaux, Morgan, 111
Morano, Barbara, 6
Mounting of artwork, 49–50, 105
Museum of Modern Art (New York City), 30
Museums, 38, 75–76, 80, 81, 96, 97–98, 102, 106, 122. See also specific museum

Narrative themes, 17, 33, 112–13
National Art Education Association (NAEA), 89, 97, 147–49
Natrona County School District (Wyoming), 34, 120
New Art Center (Massachusetts), 19, 114, 115
North Haven Public Schools (Connecticut), 107, 145

Offensive art, 90–92
Openings, 4, 20, 44, 65, 72, 76–77, 106, 108, 134–35. See also Receptions
Originality, 90
Orleans Elementary School (Massachusetts), 27, 118–19
Oulevy, Christine, 145

Parents, 68, 76, 89, 93, 116, 140; and benefits of exhibits, 6, 108; and empty spaces as places for art, 106; and offensive art, 91, 93; permissions from, 94–95, 98, 106, 138; and support for exhibits, 96, 97, 98, 99; as viewers, 64; as volunteers, 96–97, 119

Park, Charlotte, 126

Park School (Maryland), 89, 137

Patrons, 71–72, 138

Performance art, 52–53, 58, 60–61, 63, 77

Photographic documentation, 77–79

Pickett, Michelle. See Wilson-Pickett, Michelle

Planning, 40, 46. See also Briefs; Schedules; Timetables

Posters, 65, 66, 67, 68, 116–17

Preparing artwork, 47, 49–50, 55

Press releases, 65, 67–68, 130–31

Privacy issues, 107

Programs, 71–72, 87–88, 97

Prompts, 55, 60, 71

Provenance, 47

Public. See Publicity; Viewers

Publicity, 12, 74, 88, 93, 108; and advertising, 66–68; and assessment, 72, 81; case studies about, 130–33; costs of, 98; and cultivating an audience, 65–66; and design, 64, 65, 66, 123, 124–25; and exposition, 68–72; forms of, 65; and installation, 55, 64, 65, 66, 70–71; and point of view of viewers, 64–65; as step in exhibition process, 2, 3–4, 64–73; and support for exhibits, 97, 98; and teamwork, 31, 65; and themes, 20, 64, 65, 68, 70, 71, 111

Quidor, John, 112, 113

Rao, April, 21, 116–17

Rauch, K., 105

Reams Road Elementary School (Virginia), 103, 140

Receptions, 86, 98, 119; amenities at, 76, 85; and assessment, 81, 82, 85; and docents, 75–76; and empty spaces as places for art, 101, 105; and opening program, 76–77; overview about, 74–75, 85; and photographic and video documentation, 77–79; and publicity, 67, 71, 72; and support for exhibits, 97, 98

Refreshments, 76, 85, 105

Regional shows, 104–5

Reich, Lilly, 29–30

Resources, 34. See also Budget

Retrospectives, 16, 21, 116–17

Returning artwork, 80, 138, 142–43

Reviews, 4, 65, 69, 72–73, 131–32

Rhythm, 37

Rituals, 58, 61

Robben, Karen, 86

Rosenquist, James, 131

Ross School (New York), 15, 16, 35, 36, 56, 62, 69–70, 72, 88, 111–12, 121–22, 126, 128–29, 131–33

Rubrics: assessment, 83; and selection of art, 23–24, 28

Sabol, Robert, 38, 39, 79, 82, 124–25

Safety concerns, 93, 94

Salon-style design, 26, 29, 33–34, 46, 120–25

Sanchez, Diego, 83

Sanders Gallery, 123

Saugatuck, Michigan, 98, 138

Scale models, 44–45

Schedules, 87–88, 90. See also Timetables

Schools: empty spaces in, 99–107; events at, 66, 100, 103, 140; exchange of artwork among, 80, 95, 105; exhibiting throughout, 103, 140–41; galleries in, 101–2, 139; hallway exhibits in, 100–101, 138–39, 140; mission of, 91

Schoolwide shows, 103–4

Schwartz, Sheri, 145

Sears, Autumn, 21, 117–18
Security, 95–96, 107, 137
Selection of artwork, 62, 64, 88, 121, 138, 140, 143; case studies about, 126; and confrontational art, 93, 94; criteria for, 21–27, 28, 89, 93; and empty spaces as places for art, 104, 106; and events and assessment, 74, 81, 84; and juried shows and competitions, 89, 90; and legal considerations, 94; and themes, 14, 21–27, 28, 111, 112, 118–19
Selling student artwork, 97–99
Semmel, Joan, 111
Sequential design, 35, 46, 121–22
Serrell, B., 55
Sheesley, Mary Frank, 105, 141–43
"Shows in a box," 141
Signage, 47, 53, 54–55, 65, 79, 123
Sikora, M., 59
Sikora, Sherrie, 34–35, 121
Site: preparation of, 50–53
Slotnick, Ruth, 19, 114
Smith College, 139
Snow Library Gallery (Massachusetts), 118–19
Snowden, Sherry, 101, 138–39
Social dynamics, 4–6, 26–27, 93, 127
Social issues, 21, 26–27, 98–99
Social skills, 5–6, 104
Sorchik, Diane, 95
Sousa, Jean, 17, 112, 113, 128
Space: and design, 30–31, 33, 34; empty, 99–107; preparing, 47, 50–53; scale model of, 44–45; and selection of art, 26; and theme development, 26
Sponsors, 71–72, 76, 97
Staniszewski, M. A., 30
Storage, 27
Storytelling, 15–17, 76–77. See also Didactic themes
Strong-Cuevas, Elizabeth, 132–33
Sully Plantation Museum, 122
Sutton, Carolyn, 89, 137
Swift Creek Elementary School (Virginia), 127

Symbolism, 17–19, 32, 44–45, 91. See also Metaphorical themes
Synoptic design, 32, 37–38, 46, 123–24
Szekely, George, 103, 140–41

Taylor, B., 99
Teachers: roles of, 11, 12, 64, 86–87, 103, 134–35
Teaching art exhibition: case studies about, 137–45; and controversial art, 90–94; and developing a program, 87–88; and empty spaces as places for art, 99–107; and juried shows and competitions, 89–90; and legal considerations, 94–96; and originality, 90; role of teacher in, 86–87; and support for exhibits, 96–99; and working with artists, 88–89
Teamwork: and composition of teams, 39–40; and design, 31; and events and assessment, 31, 75; and installation, 31, 55, 57–58, 127; and publicity, 31, 65; and rotating members of teams, 25, 39–40, 56, 108; and selection of art, 27; and theme development, 11–14, 22, 27
Terrell, Paul Jr., 68, 130–31
Text, 47, 54–55, 61, 81, 111
Themes, 40, 86, 88, 90, 107; and ambience, 63; case studies about, 111–19; categories of, 14–21, 25, 28; and confrontational art, 93, 94; curating of, 11–12; and design, 20, 26, 28, 31–32, 33, 34, 38, 46, 120, 123, 124; development of, as step of exhibition, 2, 3, 11–28; and empty spaces as places for art, 103, 106; and events and assessment, 74, 76, 81, 84, 85, 111–12; importance of, 3, 13, 26, 27, 28; and installation, 51, 54, 55, 60–61, 62, 63; and publicity, 64, 65, 68, 70, 71, 111; and selection of art, 21–27, 28; and social dynamics of exhibitions, 5, 6, 26–27; sources of ideas for, 12–13; and teamwork and consensus building, 11–14

Thorne, Nori, 61
3-D art, 52, 58–59, 94, 114
Timetables, 3, 11, 12, 30–31, 34, 41–44, 46, 58, 65, 80. *See also* Schedules
Titles, 53–54
Toledo Museum of Art (Ohio), 77
Tommy Smith Elementary School (Florida), 141–42
Trio Sarajevo, 117–18
Turner, Janet, 53

United States Society for Education Through Art (USSEA), 141

Video documentation, 77–79
Viewers, 6, 90, 103; and assessment/feedback, 81–82, 85; and confrontational art, 92, 93; cultivating, 65–66; and design, 30–31, 35–36, 46; and events and assessment, 74–79, 85; and interactive installation, 59–60, 63, 70–71, 128; taking point of view of, 64–65; and theme development, 11, 13, 26–27; training of, 75

Virginia Museum of Fine Arts, 38, 123
Volunteers, 96–97, 105, 119

Wachusett Regional High School (Massachusetts), 102, 139
Wade, Charles Paget, 34
Wale, Ilona, 104–5
Walker, Sydney, 20, 111
Walpole High School (Massachusetts), 71
Walton, C., 77
Weisman, E., 13
Westgarth, Ralph, 106, 144–45
Wheeler, S., 30
"White cube" style, 30
Wichita, Kansas, 20, 114–16
Wilson-Pickett, Michelle, 15, 111–12
Wilson, Robert, 105
Wise, Christa, 98, 138
Wood, Margaret, 38, 123
www.pictureframes.com, 50
Wylder, Viki Thompson, 106, 143–44

Youth Art Month, 79, 103, 104, 118–19, 139

About the Author

David Burton is a professor in the Department of Art Education at Virginia Commonwealth University, in Richmond, Virginia, where he has taught for 28 years. He is currently the Higher Education Director of the National Art Education Association (NAEA) and the treasurer of the Virginia Art Education Association.

In 2000, he received the NAEA Higher Education Art Educator Award, and in 1997 he was awarded the NAEA Student Chapter Sponsor Award for Excellence. He has served as the secretary of the Seminar for Research in Art Education (SRAE), as the Task Force Chair for Demographic Research on the NAEA Research Commission, and as a reviewer for *Studies in Art Education*. In 2005, Burton was elected as a NAEA Distinguished Fellow.

Beginning in 2000, Burton collaborated with Read Diket and Robert Sabol on a secondary analysis of the *1997 National Assessment of Educational Progress (NAEP) Visual Arts Report Card*. The articles based on that analysis and published in *Studies in Art Education* subsequently received the 2003 Barkan Award for research in art education.

Burton has published 25 articles in scholarly journals, presented more than 50 papers at national art education conventions, and more than 70 papers at state conferences over the years.